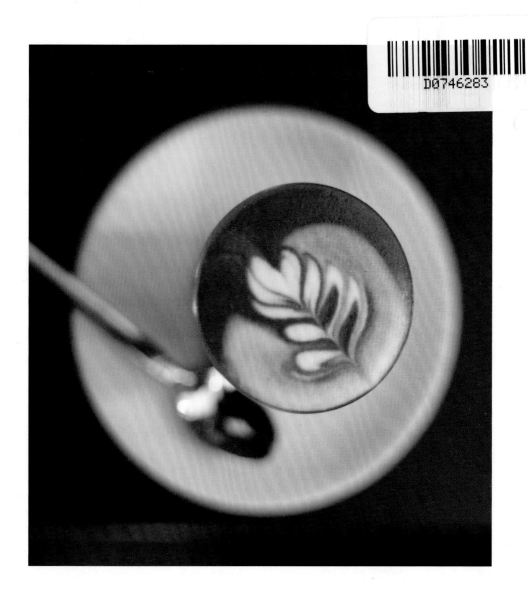

JAVA BEACH

1396

café life
SAN FRANCISCO

A Guide to the City's Neighborhood Cafés

by Joe Wolff

photography by Roger Paperno

Interlink Books

First published in 2012 by

INTERLINK BOOKS
An imprint of Interlink Publishing Group, Inc.
46 Crosby Street, Northampton, Massachusetts 01060
www.interlinkbooks.com

Library of Congress Cataloging-in-Publication Data

Wolff, Joe.
 Café life San Francisco : a guidebook to the city's neighborhood cafés / text by Joe Wolff ; photos by Roger Paperno. — 1st American ed.
    p. cm.
 ISBN 978-1-56656-847-0 (pbk.)
 1. Coffeehouses—California—San Francisco—Guidebooks. I. Paperno, Roger. II. Title.
 TX907.3.C22S368 2012
 647.95794'61—dc22
                           2011008435

Printed and bound in China

To request our 48-page full-color catalog, please visit our website at: www.interlinkbooks.com, call us toll-free at: 1-800-238-LINK, or write to us at: Interlink Publishing, 46 Crosby Street, Northampton, MA 01060
e-mail: info@interlinkbooks.com

To Reba, my pretty redheaded daughter,
who knows the magic of San Francisco.
JW

To my mother, who always encouraged my dreams.
RP

CONTENTS

San Francisco

PACIFIC
OCEAN

Golden Gate
Bridge

Doyle Dr.

101

THE PRESID

Sea
Cliff

West Pacific

Lake St.

California St.

Clement St.

Lincoln Blvd

Park Presidio Blvd.

Pt. Lobos Ave.

Geary Blvd.

25th Ave.

19th Ave.

10th Ave.

8th Ave.

4th Ave.

Anza St.

34th Ave.

30th St.

28th St.

Balboa St.

Richmond

Balboa St.

43rd Ave.

Cabrillo St.

Fulton St.

Kennedy Dr.

Middle Dr. W.

GOLDEN GATE PARK

Lincoln Way

Irving St.

Inner
Sunset

Parnassu

Judah St.

Sunset Blvd.

30th St.

28th St.

10th Ave.

7th Ave.

Kirkham St.

Lawton St.

41st St.

West of
Twin
Peaks

Noriega St.

19th Ave.

Ortega St.

Sunset

Great Hwy.

Quintara St.

Forest
Hill

14th Ave.

39th St.

34th Ave.

28th St.

Dewey Blvd.

Upper Great Hwy.

Taraval St.

Taraval St.

Ulloa St.

Parkside

West
Portal

Vicente St.

Sunset Blvd.

Portola Dr.

0 1 kilometer

0 1 mile

⑫ ⑯ ⑲

⑬

①

①

⑬

⑭

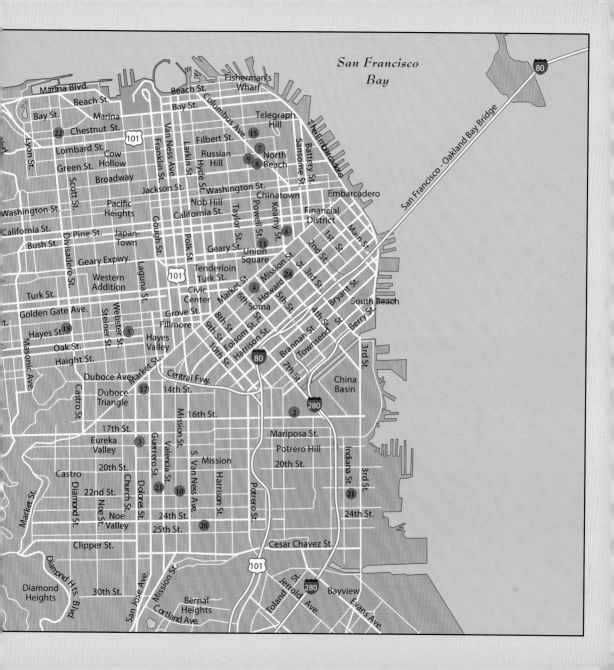

INTRODUCTION

San Francisco has many nicknames—you should know which ones to use and which ones to avoid before visiting. City by the Bay is okay. Not good are Frisco (never), San Fran, and Baghdad by the Bay (obviously). The latter is a nickname conjured up by the late, great, highly revered San Francisco newspaper columnist Herb Caen back in the early 1940s. The City by the Bay or plain San Francisco are fine. Best is "the City"—as in, "I've got a meeting in the City" or "I live in the City, near Ocean Beach." This is what the locals call it, and by using this term, you'll maximize your cool.

Ironically, you'll also increase your cool by not wearing shorts around town during the cool summers. Shorts suggest you are one of the bridge-and-tunnel people from Walnut Creek (god forbid) or Marin (better, but still not the City). These folks tend to forget about the temperature swing between fog-shrouded SF and the rest of the world, which can be as much as 30 to 40 degrees Fahrenheit in August.

Now that we have dispensed with that important information, you can begin your exploration of the City aided by *Café Life San Francisco*. As you know, San Francisco is small, only 47 square miles, and the downtown area and environs make for a charming, easy-walking little metropolis. Take it slow and explore the city center, or for the ambitious, with good walking shoes, you can hoof it from Union Square through Chinatown to North Beach, then down to the Embarcadero along the waterfront to Aquatic Park, Fort Mason, and the Presidio.

Whatever the route, you'll be traveling on your stomach, and we've got you covered in the sustenance department, with cafés from a cross section of neighborhoods: Sunset, Mission, Dogpatch, Mission Bay, Downtown, North Beach, and outside the city in the wilds of Marin County. For the most part, these establishments feature locally grown food, artisan pastries, and good coffee. We chose them because we felt comfortable there. And we liked the owners—many of them creative people who woke up one morning and decided to roast

artisan coffee or make gelato or open a neighborhood café by Ocean Beach. Luckily for you, they prevailed against all odds. (The food business is tough.) This is a testament to the creative spirit of the San Francisco Bay Area.

So go ahead—get out there. Walk, eat, and drink your way around the City, and discover its soul. But before you do, here are some people who helped make all of this possible. We'll start with Joe's daughter Reba, a pretty red-haired woman who has been an awesome guide and advance person, suggesting just the right places. Then there's our agent Julie Hill, who did what agents do and made the *Café Life* series a reality. Thanks also to our eagle-eye copyeditor Elise O'Keefe and our Italian language proofreader Costanzo Buzzelli. And, a big "thank you" from Joe to his wife Robin for her love and support during this project.

· 1 ·

DOWNTOWN

W hether you shop 'til you drop in the high-end retail temples around Union Square, or go across nearby Market Street to check out the Old Mint and the Yerba Buena Center, here are some good (strategically located) places to chill, hang, eat, and drink.

Emporio Rulli Il Caffè

On Union Square at Stockton and Post streets
7:30AM–7PM, daily
Closed Thanksgiving and Christmas Day
www.rulli.com

Ristobar
2300 Chestnut Street (at Scott Street)
(415) 923-6464
5PM–10PM, Monday to Thursday
5PM–11PM, Friday & Saturday
5PM–10PM, Sunday
www.ristobarsf.com

For Emporio Rulli in Larkspur, see pages 201–212.

Gary Rulli opened his pasticceria/café in Larkspur on Thanksgiving Day in 1988. In the Outside the City section of this book, you can read about his journey from high school kid making doughnuts to apprentice with top Italian pastry chefs, to master pasticciere creating some of the finest and most authentic Italian pastries on the planet.

But why not go one better and add a little sensual pleasure to your life by visiting the Emporio Rulli Il Caffè at Union Square, a minimalist, quarter-moon-shaped Italian bar. It offers outdoor seating, and a nice spot to people watch in the heart of San Francisco.

If Il Caffè seems to be airlifted directly from Italy and dropped into place at the end of Union Square, that's pretty much what happened. "The interior of every one of our stores has been prebuilt in Italy and then brought over here," said Gary. Italians are masterful at

remodeling small retail spaces—the builders come in, measure the store, and construct the new interior in their warehouse. They then take it apart and reconstruct it on the premises, interfering with business as little as possible. For example, they can remove an old bar and install a new one in about a week.

The design and décor of all the Rulli cafés is Gary's vision. For its implementation, he worked with an Italian company called Gelostandard (and their designer, Mario Papi), the same company responsible for the look of many grand cafés in Florence, Torino, and Milan, along with the famous Giolitti gelateria in Rome.

Another Rulli location you should visit is the Ristobar (as in ristorante/bar) in the Marina District. While not actually downtown, it's not far and offers a casual, comfortable neighborhood gathering place, where you can enjoy rustic Italian fare and artisanal pizza, along with good Italian beer and wine.

Gary has teamed up with head chef Angelo Auriana for this rendition of *un'esperienza culinaria eccellente* (exceptional food). Chef Auriana's style focuses on simple, fresh ingredients that allow each dish to reveal its natural flavors, as in the best Italian cooking. Start with *affettati* (sliced specialty salami), local producer Fra' Mani's coarse ground salami, cured with red wine and spices; *felino*, a classic Italian salami made from selected lean pork meat; or *finocchiona*, seasoned with fennel, white pepper, and garlic. Add a few slices of *formaggio* (cheese) that you don't run into every day, such as *Raschera* from Piemonte, a semi-smooth texture with imprints of cheesecloth on the rind; or *mandriano di zambla*, delicate and fragrant, produced in Lombardia near the Swiss border.

Moving on to salads, how about one of the following: *puntarelle*, chicory, *burrata* (a buttery mozzarella), bell peppers, and anchovy dressing; *indivia bianca* with endive, watercress, candied walnuts, and clementines; or *sardoni*, marinated sardines, tiny tomatoes, arugula, and salsa verde.

If you never ate your broccoli as a kid, that's a thing of the past with *broccoli piccanti*—sautéed broccolini, garlic, and shredded peperoncini. Next try a plate of tender gnocchi, dressed with gorgonzola dolce latte and Sicilian pistachios.

The Ristobar also serves up a tasty pizza. Try the Market Street, with smoked mozzarella, escarole, Calabrian chili, and herbs or the Valencia, topped with goat cheese, asiago, pears, and watercress.

Main courses include *gamberoni* (sea bass wrapped prawns, arugula, *bottarga di muggine*); *orata* (olive oil, poached sea bream, lemon, olive tapenade); and *polpettine* or lamb meatballs with raisins, almonds, zucchini sauce.

Any room left? If not, you better find some for *affogato al caffè*, made with Rulli's Il Golosone Espresso, gelato al mascarpone, and whipped cream; *tropicale*, large pearl tapioca and coconut milk with passion fruit cream; or *budino di panettone*, a panettone bread pudding topped with vanilla gelato.

The Ristobar décor has a rich masculine feel similar to the Gilli, Rivoire, and Paszkowski cafés in Florence. If you're inclined to lean back in your chair and stare at the ceiling fresco, go ahead and indulge. It's the work of Venetian artist Carlo Marchiori, who lives in Calistoga, California. Marchiori studied art and design in Italy before moving to Canada, where he worked as a film animator and an illustrator. One of his animated shorts earned an Academy Award nomination in 1967. Eventually he left the world of filmmaking and advertising to concentrate on painting. Not surprisingly, his work combines a classic approach with the freshness of modern media.

The playful, elegant ceiling mural in the Ristobar tells the story of its food, wine, and pastry—using chef-acrobats and jugglers. (One of these characters is even walking a tightrope across the ceiling.) This is the second Carlo Marchiori artwork commissioned by Gary, the first being a wall mural in the Larkspur café.

"An Italian lady introduced me to Carlo years ago, when I said I wanted to do the Larkspur mural. Seven pastry chefs were coming over from Italy for the Columbus Day celebration in 1992. A lot of them were my mentors from Italy," said Gary. "I was talking to Carlo and said, 'Why don't we do something with the eight pastry chefs?' He suggested a gondola on a canal with all the chefs inside. One is putting panettone in a brick oven. Another's rolling out marzipan. Another sleeping. It's very fun and whimsical. He's also got my wife as the lady under the umbrella, and my son Giancarlo."

Emporio Rulli Il Caffè is a genuine Italian bar in the heart of the city. Sit outside and enjoy good panini, pastry, vino, and coffee. The coffee is like you get in Italy. In fact, an Italian tourist was observed at the Union Square location taking a sip of an espresso and remarking with great surprise, "Questo è buono!" (This is good.) She had obviously experienced many bad coffees during her visit to America. If so inclined, head over to Rulli's Ristobar in the Marina District for a fine meal of simple, tasty, rustic fair.

Café Metropol

**168 Sutter Street (between Kearny Street
and Lick Place)**
(415) 732-7777
11AM–9PM, Monday to Friday
7AM–2PM, Saturday
Closed Sunday
www.cafe-metropol.com

That tall, charming, Austrian guy who greets you warmly at the door of Café Metropol is not actually the doorman. He's Klaus Ranier, one of the owners. Both he and his older brother, Albert, run a family business that includes Metropol and usually one other place (presently, they are between second restaurants). Klaus and Albert are so gracious they could operate a charm school for restaurateurs. Nothing forced or feigned with these two—the secret behind their approach is simple: they really like what they're doing.

"I treat people like I want to be treated," explains Klaus. "If I spend money and the waitress and maître d' acknowledge me, it makes me feel good. So why shouldn't I do that in my own business? I think people appreciate it, especially in San Francisco, where there are lots of good restaurants with high-quality food."

Their idea was to create a European-style café/bistro, with a casual atmosphere where you can enjoy a cup of coffee and a slice of cake, or a nice lunch—and after work, a nice stiff martini with your colleagues. "In this neighborhood, it's either very upscale or small delis.

So, we came in with a different concept, and after all these years, it has been very successful," Klaus explained. In an area where a restaurant's life span is often short, Café Metropol has flourished since it opened in 1992. (To the brothers, the name Metropol signifies being in the city at the center of things.)

Before Café Metropol, the space was home to a failed bistro with glass-topped tables, funky chairs, neon lights, hard colors, and an absentee owner. When Klaus and Albert took over, they softened the look and feel, adding soft hanging lights, warm tones, and large flower displays. "We never want to be the hot spot. Consistently good and build a nice customer base—that's our goal," said Klaus, who spends more time at Metropol than his brother.

"We have a lot of regular customers. Some come in everyday, and many come in at least once a week. I have a nice clientele—I'd say 85 percent are people who work here in the financial district. In San Francisco, people are very educated when it comes to food. You don't get away with too much. You have to be consistently good," continued Klaus. "I certainly appreciate return customers, but sometimes I think, 'There are so many other restaurants, why do you come here every day?' But they really enjoy it, which means we must be doing something right."

Klaus takes care of his regulars—if they're in the mood for a piece of swordfish, for example, and it's not on the menu, he'll serve it up for them. He also likes to hear what people think, even criticism. "If someone says, 'Hey, I didn't like the soup much today,' I appreciate that. Regulars tell you right away. This keeps us on our toes," he explained.

During the summertime, when many of the regulars are on vacation, European tourists fill the gaps at Metropol. Many of them are, surprisingly, not very adventuresome. They take the cautious route, ordering pizza margarita and cappuccino from a colorful menu that offers so much more. While Klaus appreciates the patronage of these visitors, he said, "I'm happy to have my group of regulars back at the end of the summer. They know what they like, and they appreciate what they get."

What they get are good seasonal dishes: lots of local organic greens in the summer and heartier fare in the winter—with specials that change every day. Here are some examples of why Café Metropol has a big following: the not-too-creamy salmon chowder containing applewood smoked bacon, fresh roasted salmon, and toasted croutons, which combine to give a creamy, crunchy texture. (There's also a little bite to the finish.) The fresh ahi tuna tartar (marinated in lemon juice, olive oil, chives, parsley, and basil) over fresh avocado with homemade potato chips offers a sashimi-like freshness. Also, try the flat iron steak, sautéed in herb butter and reduced wine sauce, mashed potatoes on the side, or the café meatloaf, cradled in applewood smoked bacon, nestled on garlic mashed potatoes and mixed vegetables.

Maybe you're after something a little more streamlined, such as the tarragon chicken salad sandwich—tomato, arugula, and chopped chicken, held captive by a thin slice of salami and a thin slice of swiss cheese, on housemade three-grain bread; the pork fajita sandwich with chipotle aioli, baby arugula, and pepper jack cheese; or a pizza with salami, caramelized onions, cherry tomatoes, artichoke, spinach, and mozzarella.

Afterward, savor a slice of light, yet sinful, ricotta cheesecake, which is more like cake than the typical heavy American-style cheesecake, and slightly grainy so you really taste the ricotta. The focaccia and whole grain breads are baked daily, using organic flour.

"I'm here every day, always in the kitchen, tasting everything," said Klaus. "Albert helps me out with the menu, but mostly I design it. I love food, so when I go to other restaurants, I get ideas about what chefs are doing there. This inspires me, and then I put my own signature on a dish.

"The food and drink business is like the fashion industry. For example, Pomtinis (vodka plus pomegranate, grapefruit, and lime juice) are in right now. During the summer, raspberry and peach mojitos sold like crazy. You always have to be out there finding out what's going on, which is fun."

After Klaus creates a dish, his kitchen staff executes it. Most have been with him for a long time. "When we do something new, we cook it together. They are talented young guys, and they do it the way I like it," Klaus says. "When the customers like one of our new dishes, this inspires us. It makes everyone feel good."

There are many long-time employees at Metropol—eighteen years for the pastry maker, and twelve years for some of the wait staff. "Most have been here at least five years. Everyone understands that we have to work hard, but we have fun," said Klaus.

Klaus and Albert grew up in a home where mom served good simple food. There were no soft drinks on the table— they got a Coca-Cola only at Christmas. The bacon, ham, milk, and eggs came from small neighboring farms, and the vegetables grew in their own garden. It was all natural, the precursor of slow food and California cuisine.

The backdrop for this hearty and healthy fare was the small town of Langau at 6,000 feet in the Austrian Alps, just outside Salzburg. Their mom ran a tree nursery and dad was a lumberjack. Whenever Klaus returns for a visit, he feels very lucky that he grew up there. At a certain point, however, wanderlust kicked in for both him and Albert, and they figured the hotel/

restaurant business was a good way to explore the world. (After living among the pines, Klaus says that he had a strong desire to see palm trees.)

Albert trained as a chef and worked in some very good Salzburg restaurants before taking a job in San Francisco. Klaus studied to be a pastry chef, and then, after his internship, worked in well-known hotels such as the Gstaad Palace in Gstaad and the Hotel Sacher in Salzburg, as well as high-end restaurants in Germany.

Klaus eventually found his dream job aboard a floating hotel—the Cunard Lines's *Sagafjord*. "Sometimes when I think I'd like a change, I close my eyes and remember the fun days on the cruise ship. I was much younger, and it was a lot of hard work, but almost every day I was in a different and beautiful spot."

"It was not a huge ship. We had 400 to 500 passengers. We worked in the morning, and then in the afternoon, we went ashore. I got to see a lot of places that otherwise I would never have seen. Also, you're carefree. You have great food, a place to stay, and cash in your pocket. Life is good. There's a built-in social life with the 300 crew members, who are all between 20 and 40 years old. And lots of parties: birthday parties, farewell parties, welcome-back parties. We worked hard and played harder. You work for four or five months and take two or three months off.

"I miss the traveling. We'd go from South America all the way to the North Cape in Norway. I pretty much went around the world," Klaus continued.

Not long after Klaus came aboard, his talent was recognized and he became executive pastry chef, which meant that he had ship's officer status and his own cabin.

It happened like this, explained Klaus: "Even though I was fairly young, I had a great resume. When the executive pastry chef went on vacation and the sous chef took over, the ratings plummeted. He just couldn't handle the job. The food and beverage director had a meltdown. So I said, 'Let me try. I think I can do it.' I took over, and I was full of energy. We did new dishes. The ratings went way up.

"When the executive pastry chef came back, the food and beverage director fired him because my ratings were much better. It was sad because I got along with him very well.

After this experience I said to myself, 'Klaus, you to need think about moving on, getting more experience. You don't want to be here in 15 years and have some young kid come along and kick your ass.'"

Later, the ship went into dry dock and Klaus came to San Francisco to visit his brother Albert, something he did whenever he had the chance. Klaus was always smitten with the City, but this time, he fell deeply in love. After three years at sea, he decided to stay and found a job at the Fairmont Hotel.

"When I came to San Francisco, it was nice to have someone from my own family here. It made things much easier in a new culture," said Klaus. Spending time together in the City by the Bay gave the brothers a chance to bond in a way that was not possible when they were younger. Albert is six years older than Klaus, and he'd left home at sixteen to attend hotel school and to work.

Klaus said, with a sly grin, "He's the older brother. He always knows better. Is Albert always right? Of course."

"We have our small disagreements," continued Klaus, "but we do make a good team. We think the same way, and complement each other. Over the years, Albert likes to do more of the business part. He likes to work out deals, and look after the financial side. And I'm more the creative side. I like to be in the kitchen creating new dishes. Or be in the dining room, talking with the customers to make sure everything is going well. I like the daily operations. For me, it is torture if you put me in the office and say, 'Hey, take care of this pile of papers.' You would kill me slowly. I need to be around food, wine and people."

Klaus and Albert's dream had always been to own a restaurant, which they finally realized with the Hyde Street Bistro, a small neighborhood trattoria/bistro that was very successful. This was followed by Café Metropol, along with a couple of other places. "The city has treated us well, and now it has turned out to be home," said Klaus. (Albert arrived in 1985 and Klaus in 1989.)

Like many residents of the Bay Area, Klaus feels fortunate to live in a place that has so much to offer: an ideal Mediterranean climate, a variety of cultures, the Pacific Ocean and Sierra Nevada mountains a stone's throw away, an amazing array of fresh produce and artisan food, and the wine country right next door. "We are very, very spoiled," said Klaus. "Sometimes I think maybe I should move back to Europe, and then I spend three weeks there, and think, no. On vacation, I talk to people, and they dread going home, but I don't mind going home at all. I'm very happy to be living here."

As for travel, when Klaus has more time, he usually plans a trip back to Austria to see his mother. For a shorter getaway and restorative vacation, he heads down to Central or South America for some scuba diving and a dose of the tropical climes. He has zeroed in on Belize and Honduras for the past few years, and especially a small island called Roaton, off the northern coast of Honduras.

"I go down there for at least a week. People know me there. They're kind of my lost family—they're always very excited when they see me," explains Klaus. "I like to go scuba diving by myself because I'm always around people. On vacation, I like to let things unfold a little bit."

People tell the Ranier brothers that they're lucky to have a good business, and Klaus agrees that luck is involved, but a lot of their success is plain hard work. His mantra: "Be consistent and greet the people. Show them you're there every day, and that you care."

Located on the cusp of the financial district and Union Square with all its retail temples, Café Metropol is mostly patronized by people who work in the area. This doesn't mean there is no room for you. Owners and brothers Klaus and Albert Ranier welcome everyone. They're fun, charming guys. The food is tasty, and they're open for both lunch and dinner. You can also drop in anytime for sweets and coffee; in this case, try a slice of Klaus's special, light ricotta cheesecake.

Samovar Tea Lounge

Yerba Buena Gardens, Upper Terrace
730 Howard Street
(415) 227-9400
10AM–8PM, Sunday to Wednesday
10AM–9PM, Thursday to Saturday
www.samovarlife.com

From the very beginning, Jesse Jacobs was steeped in tea culture like oolong in a fine china pot. He describes the Boston household where he grew up as "an eclectic liberal family with many international visitors. The ritual of drinking tea was a part of life for the Chinese, Japanese, European, and Indian people living with us. It was always a part of my childhood."

Jesse graduated from the University of Massachusetts at Amherst and also studied in both Denmark and Japan, countries where tea forms an important part of the lifestyle. This is especially true for the Danish folk schools or *hojskole*. These "schools for life," which offer no vocational or professional training, are open to everyone over the age of 18. Jesse spent a year and half at a folk school in the Jutland area of Denmark.

"People can leave their daily life of work, marriage, school, family and go to these schools to study without any academic evaluation: no grades, no competition," said Jesse. "The school was out in the country, in the middle of nowhere. Every Sunday was set aside for drinking herbal tea and just talking, about politics, about life, about whatever."

N.F.S. Grundtvig (1783–1872), a Danish minister, poet, and philosopher, started the folk school movement in the 1830s. Although he didn't actually found any schools himself, his disciples opened a total of 50 Danish folk schools between 1850 and 1870. Grundtvig thought education should be available to everyone, not just the elite.

Each folk school is state supported through public grants and designs its own curriculum—an amazing variety of subjects, such as art, music, ecology, travel, foreign languages, ethnic cooking, and agriculture. Over the years, folk schools have even specialized in ultraconservative Christian theology, the interests of retired people, and transcendental meditation.

Jesse also spent a year in Japan, studying Japanese culture, history, and political science, along with Zen archery and martial arts. And he continued stirring the (tea) pot by teaching English in exchange for tea ceremony classes. "I really got into the whole Zen world," he said.

His next move, after starting a web development company in the Boston area: a cross-country drive to California for the high-tech boom, where he worked with two start-up companies in the Bay Area.

He said the moment of truth came when he was in Seattle developing software applications for a Fortune 500 company. "It was a cold, drizzly, icy day. I looked up and saw cubicle farms everywhere and said, 'Man, that's it.' I wanted to wake up and know I had a reason beyond a paycheck. I wanted to live my life around people I relate to and connect to," explained Jesse.

"Now what?" Jesse asked himself, "If I could do anything, what would that be?" He loved the City, organic food, and tea. And he knew there was nowhere in San Francisco that offered the type of tea experience he wanted, someplace hip, relaxed, and sophisticated, where he could take his grandmother. So he decided to create his own modern interpretation of a teahouse.

Of course, this required some dough (and a few partners). Jesse talked to his friends Paul Fullarton and Robert Sandler. The three of them pooled savings, put a business plan together, and went searching for a loan. They split up the responsibilities. Jesse's job was to cold call a list of 75 banks.

He heard "no" 74 times in six months. The refrain was familiar: you have no experience, no collateral, and no one has done this before. Then, the three entrepreneurs met with the last bank on the list. Jesse made *pu-erh* tea for the lending officer, and he was blown away by the quality and the exotic nature of the experience. "I just think it might work. I'm going to sign off on it," he said. "Who knows, I could be losing my job over this, but you know what, I believe in you." Good call.

On June 5, 2003, the first Samovar Tea Lounge opened at 18th and Sanchez in what was a space occupied by a defunct coffee shop. "From the beginning, the goal was to create a company that would succeed based on the value of the experience," said Jesse. Little by little the business found its feet and a following, and after four years, the City of San Francisco came to the Samovar three and said, "We have a location in Yerba Buena Gardens that used to be a Starbucks (ironically). It didn't fly. We think tea in the garden would be great. A lot of our employees come to Samovar. Are you interested in expanding?"

They were. The only problem—once again—was money. Since there wasn't time to get an SBA loan or a traditional bank loan, they went to a peer-to-peer lending site and secured two $10,000 loans at 10 percent in a few weeks. The peer-to-peer lending concept works this way: prospective borrowers get a credit score, fill out an application, and then pitch lenders on their idea, the amount needed, and proposed interest rate.

Since expanding to the second location in Yerba Buena Gardens, Robert and Paul returned to the full-time corporate world. They are, however, still involved in spirit. Jesse remains operating partner and founder of Samovar.

In case you're not sure what or where Yerba Buena Gardens are—they're a two-block area of public parks in the center of San Francisco, bordered by Mission and Folsom, and Third and Fourth streets. Highlights include grassy meadows, trees, flowers, and public art (such as the spectacular Martin Luther King, Jr. Memorial with its 50-foot-high waterfall). On the upper terrace, you can enjoy a pot of tea at Samovar and look out on the gardens— and the world. Yerba Buena, San Francisco's original name, means "good herb"—referring to wild mint that grew in the hills surrounding the 1835 settlement of 460 people (who lived in tents, adobes, and shanties).

It may be surprising to learn that the goal of Samovar is not really to sell tea. "It is to create peace," said Jesse. "Tea is simply the vehicle." One of Jesse's friends met Abbie Hoffman (1936–1989), the 1960s political activist, shortly before he died. This notorious founder of the Yippie movement and one of the Chicago Seven said to Jesse's friend, "Don't tell anyone, but I really believe business is the best tool for social change."

"This resonated with me," explained Jesse. "I thought, wow. I can make a difference. Someone can come in feeling upset about whatever is out there, have a half hour to relax, and then walk out in the world. And we've made a difference. That's very profound—and feasible." Jesse wants Samovar Tea Lounge to offer an escape from the day-to-day, a place to have a little bit of peace (in a world full of chaos)—without forests of laptops and flocks of chirping cell phones. He feels that stillness, physical connection, and ritual are lacking in today's manic society, and he sees Samovar as a vehicle for delivering stillness through the hands-on mini-ritual of tea drinking. Coffee is fast. Tea is slow.

Most staff members flourish under Jesse's management philosophy—there are only two rules: no bad questions and no ceiling. If you want a part-time job for college, that's cool. Or, if you want to help him grow and build yourself a career, it's wide open. He wants to develop leaders so he does not have to be the critical path for everything.

A good example of Jesse's management philosophy in action is Eric, the 26-year-old operations manager. He started as a dishwasher, spoke little English, ate only burritos, hated Samovar's food, never drank tea, and brought a Coke to work. Over time, Eric wanted to make more money. Jesse told him, "You can make a little bit of money or you can make a lot. If you want to work with me, I will help you. I'm looking for people who will lead." Eric was motivated and willing to change. He learned to make the tea, then became a server, and learned how to take inventory. Before long, he was assistant manager, manager, and, finally, operations manager (a point of contact for the stores)—the go-to guy for troubleshooting a problem before bringing it to Jesse. Eric now brings his own chopsticks when he goes out to eat.

Another example of Samovar's flexible "no ceiling" policy is Diana, the cleaning lady for the coffee shop that occupied the Sanchez Street space before going out of business. During the Samovar renovations, she asked Jesse for a job, and became one of the first dishwashers. She progressed to cook and tea maker, and, eventually, moved to Yerba Buena Gardens as

a server. Her daughter, Esther, who followed a similar career path, is now the manager of the Yerba Buena Gardens tea lounge. She has even come out with a new tea blend of her own.

Jesse also tries to empower his people with open-book management—which is the concept of showing financials to employees. The idea is to get them to think like an owner rather than a hired hand.

"It's risky," said Jesse, "but if you, the employee, know the score, you can do something about it." His managers have embraced this idea. They look at everything—including how a cup and a half of Russian tea in the samovar, instead of only a cup, can affect the bottom line. On a more macro level, due to monitoring the run rate, revenue, and tea usage, Jesse's managers suggested buying 500 pounds of jasmine tea (a three-months supply) at a discounted rate, instead of 10 pounds every week. "I don't want to be the smartest one," continued Jesse. "People get smarter when you expect them to be smarter."

The Samovar Tea Lounge features a large functioning electric samovar as a centerpiece. Lest you confuse scimitar and samovar, the former is a curved sword, and the latter, a large boiler or metal urn with a metal pipe running through the middle, which originally was filled with burning charcoal or pine cones, and used to heat the water. (They're now mostly electric.) A teapot filled with concentrated tea sits on top—you dilute each glass of tea with water drawn from the faucet in the bottom of the samovar. Russians usually sweeten theirs with jam. You can do the same, or drink it undiluted for a kick-butt hit of caffeine.

There is much controversy about the samovar's origin. Some say it first came from Central Asia. Russians, however, insist that it originated in their country, in particular around Tula, which was the center of samovar making in the early 1800s. Samovars are also part of tradition in Iran, Turkey, and Poland, and according to Jesse, his Lithuanian/Russian great-grandparents always used a samovar.

The menu reads, "They say Tolstoy fueled his creativity by drinking Russian tea from the samovar. See what it does for you." Jesse offers a Russian Tea Service, which includes a bottomless cup of tea, tarragon-marinated beets, smoked whitefish and horseradish, paprika deviled eggs with caviar, rye crisps, fresh fruit, and a chocolate brownie. You'll also find tea services from other cultures: Indian, Japanese, Moroccan, English, and Chinese.

Every dish on the menu uses carefully selected ingredients and is presented with great care—from the fresh-baked cherry oat scones and polenta ginger waffles to the tasty sandwiches (check out the grilled sun-dried tomato, pesto, and agor cheese on toasted ciabatta).

Of course, the real reason you come here is for the tea—and to chill out. Choose from a variety of white, green, oolong, black, *pu-erh*, and herbal teas. As Jesse's tea menu points out, "We purchase our tea fresh, every season, from small family farms and estates around the world. These people do sustainable farming, and produce incredible teas for us." Many of these teas are certified Fair Trade and USDA Organic.

All tea leaves come from the *Camellia sinensis* plant, and if you want to learn more, you'll find pretty much everything there is to know at the Learn About Tea link on the Samovar website (www.samovarlife.com).

Most tea blending takes place every Monday morning at 7AM in the Sanchez Street store. Jesse personally knows many of his suppliers, such as Wong Jian Pin and his family, who produce the fragrant Keemun Spring Down black tea. It's hand picked during a small window, usually from the end of March to the beginning of April, and then sun cured. Samovar's Shizuoka black tea comes from the Kinesuka family, the only black tea producers in Japan. Daughter Ayumi, a former customer, went to UC Berkeley and left the corporate world to return to the family tea farm. She hand delivers this tea twice a year. The same family also provides the menu's Ayumicha green tea.

"This creates something more than just serving some brown liquid. The leaf being personally selected by the family is very profound in these days of big box stores," said Jesse. "We serve a literally handcrafted product."

Samovar Tea Lounge blended a special new tea for the Dalai Lama called "Ocean of Wisdom." This soothing herbal tea is traveling around the world as part of *The Missing Peace: Artists Consider the Dalai Lama*, an exhibit of works of art inspired by the Dalai Lama and created by 88 artists from 30 countries.

Part of the Yerba Buena Samovar's calming effect comes from the décor. "I wanted a place that has texture and a lot of natural materials. A place that's warm," explained Jesse. To get this effect, he brought together a community of tea people and told them to "go crazy, I trust you, you're good at what you do."

"I worked with a local artisan who uses a lot of renewable resources, like these bamboo tables, and the recycled wood that's used on the shelves in the wall. A local woman, a friend of mine, made the drapes, and a Japanese friend designed the teapots and cups to be very functional. The lids don't fall off, and they have a good pour. The cups have holders on both sides," he adds.

You'll notice the magnificent chandeliers when you walk into this space. Jesse had them made in Taiwan, and each one weighs only 70 pounds. "We needed something that would create an atmosphere at night. They have a very sharp spotlight so just the tables are illuminated, nothing else. It creates kind of a candlelit hut."

What does Jesse do when he's not blending tea, selling tea, and nurturing his tea lounges? He spends time with his young son, Marcus, and his wife Joanna, a graphic designer who did the Samovar menus, website, and logo. In addition, believe it or not, he also practices tai chi and yoga, surfs at Ocean Beach (not for sissies), and flies his kite.

"I have a huge kite," he said. "And I like to go down to Ocean Beach. It's kind of like a truck pulling you down the street. Every so often, I get lifted up 10 to 15 feet, and then gradually land." And Jesse knows how to land—he was an NCAA gymnast in college and got into the sport because he wanted to propel his body through the air. Ask him nicely and he might do a handstand for you.

You need to calm down—and here's the perfect place. Hang out, drink tea, and listen to the waterfall. Be prepared for periods of liveliness outside, when the Yerba Buena Center has one of its fun noisy weekend festivals. You can also check out the original Samovar at Castro/Mission (18th and Sanchez) and the newest one in Hayes Valley (Page and Laguna streets). You'll find tourists, retirees, young hipsters, mothers with strollers, and traveling businessmen. Along with the occasional celebrity: Leonardo di Caprio, Rosario Dawson, and Tracy Chapman (a regular at Sanchez Street).

Blue Bottle Coffee Company

Mint Plaza Café
66 Mint Street (corner of Jessie Street)
(415) 495-3394
7AM–7PM, Monday to Friday
8AM–6PM, Saturday
8AM–4PM, Sunday

Kiosk
315 Linden Street (in Hayes Valley)
(415) 252-7535
7AM–5 or 6PM, Monday to Friday
8AM–5 or 6PM, Saturday & Sunday
www.bluebottlecoffee.net

There are many ways to make beautiful music—and James Freeman has excelled at two of them: the clarinet and the coffee bean. The unlikely owner of Blue Bottle Coffee Company made his way for years as a professional musician, playing the clarinet for a number of local orchestras including the Modesto, Napa Valley, and Monterey Symphonies.

"I'd done a lot of chamber music and new music. I did this from age 12 to 32 or 33… pretty much playing clarinet all day, every day. Eventually, I got burned out on the travel," explained James.

While on the road, James made sure that he drank good coffee using his own roasted beans, ground in a hand-cranked, old-world Zassenhaus grinder and brewed in a French press. During this time, he began to feel the rhythm of the coffee bean.

The idea to sell his roasted coffee beans to the public gravitated very slowly from crazy pipe dream to actual plan. "I shopped at the farmer's market, and I thought no one was

serving coffee there in a way that matched the quality at the market," said James. "I first sold beans for a few months, and then I bought an espresso cart, which we still have. And that's how I got our start. Inadvertently, it ended up being a smart business move because it was very low overhead."

In what was more or less a closet, he roasted beans, six pounds at a time, in a very small roaster, and then peddled them within 48 hours of roasting. His coffee had to be fresh (still his policy). And so, people who were tired of the stomach acid–inducing, San Francisco–style dark roast began to appreciate the music James was creating with his organic and shade-grown beans.

James's next step was opening the hole-in-the-wall Hayes Valley Kiosk (in 2005)—a garage neatly fitted out with a counter for dispensing espresso, drip coffee, New Orleans iced

coffee, and cookies. Hayes Valley definitely benefited from the 1989 Loma Prieta earthquake, which damaged the Hayes Street freeway ramp that cast a dark and creepy shadow over a dangerous, marginal neighborhood. The freeway ramp was torn down, and the freshly painted row houses beneath the freeway now breathe a sigh of relief. The neighborhood flourishes.

Was James satisfied with just the kiosk? Of course not—next on his list: a café, which opened its doors in 2008 at the corner of Mint and Jessie streets (a former alleyway and now a mini-plaza nestled up to the old San Francisco Mint building).

"I chose this building because I loved it. It has an identical twin in the Lower East Side of Manhattan—the Provident Savings Building. They built the one in New York in 1918, and then built this next. The landlord here is a great guy. He's seen this neighborhood at its worst," said James.

The building has had quite a history—originally it housed offices, was later abandoned, and even, at one point, inhabited by a squatter who set fire to it. Happily, the neighborhood is on its way up, and Blue Bottle has helped with the turnaround. So has the plan for the old San Francisco Mint next door (also called the Old Mint or the Granite Lady). It's in the process of being transformed into a mixed-use cultural center: part history museum, part visitor center, and part retail.

From your perch at the Blue Bottle window, look carefully at the top rear of the Old Mint building. You'll see a corner singed by the devastating fire that followed the 1906 earthquake. On April 18, things got pretty hot around this neighborhood as flames raced toward the building. The mint, along with $300 million in gold and silver (one-third of the

U.S. gold reserves and the equivalent of $6 billion today), might have been destroyed if it wasn't for the valiant stand by mint superintendent, Frank Leahy, and a few dozen men.

Built at a cost of $2 million in 1874, the Old Mint stood on a five-feet-thick granite foundation and enclosed a central courtyard with a well. This direct access to water was the main reason that the building survived the conflagration. Leahy instructed his men to soak the building's interior and roof using bucket brigades and two one-inch hoses. The heat became so intense that it burned clothes off the firefighter's backs, melted glass in the Old Mint's windows, and exploded the granite and sandstone blocks on its facing. But the fire passed through; the Old Mint prevailed. Afterward, its well continued to save the day, providing the only potable water in the area.

It is here in Blue Bottle's light, airy, renovated space with high-ceilings and tall windows that James gets to play with his collection of coffee machines, and you get to benefit from the great and varied coffee they produce.

Let's start with the siphon machine, which has a turn-of-the-19th-century, futuristic appearance. You can put one of these babies in your kitchen for around 20 grand. The siphon has been around a long time—approximately 150 years ago, it appeared in both France and Germany, although back then, they obviously didn't use halogen, as does Blue Bottle's Japanese siphon machine. It consists of the following elements: a halogen burner; a glass globe on the bottom that comes in contact with the burner; a glass globe on top with a siphon tube that fits neatly into the bottom globe and seals itself, creating a partial vacuum; and a coffee filter.

Put water in the bottom, your coffee in the top, and apply heat (but do not boil). Water is forced into the top globe with the coffee. As this happens, the barista slowly and carefully stirs the grounds with a small bamboo paddle for about 90 seconds. "There is a definite technique. You stir very gently to create a vortex or whirlpool to do most of the work," explained James. "You don't want the paddle to cut into the mass of coffee. You want the whirlpool to do most of the work. One of the marks of a good siphon barista is keeping the dome (of coffee grounds) over the filter. You want as much coffee as possible over the filter. The skill of the barista makes the difference," James says he rehearsed for months stirring plain water before he attempted a live performance with the siphon machine—a very theatrical apparatus.

Turn off the heat and the brewed coffee in the top globe is pulled down through the filter into the bottom globe, giving you a carefully brewed cup of siphon coffee. Blue Bottle's siphon bar usually features three different single-origin coffees; each delivers a pure and delicate flavor.

Another of James's machines—the Japanese Kyoto-style cold coffee maker—looks as if it was conceived in the mind's eye of Jules Verne. It works more or less like a still—drip, drip, dripping cold water very slowly down through the coffee. "The drips are about 88 beats per second," explained James. "It takes 8 to 10 hours to drip though. I feel that iced coffee needs to stay cold the whole way through. If you heat coffee and then try to chill it, it's compromised." Intense and syrupy, with a liquor finish, Kyoto-style cold coffee will appeal to your coffee purist.

In addition, your coffee "regular guy" can enjoy an espresso drink of choice made with the café's La Marzocco machine, or simply order a cup of drip coffee.

Even with the right machine, the missing link in a good coffee is often a good barista. Your average barista does not have a clue how to draw a shot or steam milk. Not the case at Blue Bottle.

"Here the barista is a high-skill position. Training is pretty extensive. Baristas start bar backing at the farmer's market. And like at music school where they have exams, we have juries for baristas. Before they can make drinks at Blue Bottle, they have to go to our roastery and make drinks for us," said James.

James moved up from the small batch roaster to a 1958 gas Probat from Germany. He likes the fact that this roaster is not automated and mostly cast iron—the latter, he feels, adds something special to the coffee's flavor. (He recently took over a 9,000-square-foot space in Oakland, expanded his headquarters and roasting facilities, and added another vintage roaster.)

The following describes a few of James's coffee compositions with the Probat, taken from the Blue Bottle website.

First, the single origin coffees:

Chiapas—"This organic Mexican coffee from the Chiapas region comes from a co-op of small, mainly indigenous landholders. It is carefully milled and processed near the growing region and beautifully sorted for export. At a single roast level, this coffee is pleasant but dainty, with sweetness but not much complexity."

Ethiopian Sidamo—"The Sidamo is a punchy, winey, dry-processed, certified organic coffee from Ethiopia, which resembles a good nonorganic Harrar, if that's helpful. In a filter or press pot, you get a deep, berry richness. As it cools, you get a lingering, but fragile poise…"

Mesa de los Santos—"This is a lovely coffee from one of the oldest, most responsible and well-run organically certified estates in Colombia. We drink it, smile gently, and scratch our heads, trying to think of a better adjective than this: 'rich.'"

Nayarita—"This is a remarkable Mexican coffee. Usually only the worst, most horrible not-for-export coffees in Mexico are dry processed (saves money on electricity for the water pump, and saves money on labor). But this is a lovingly farmed and dry-processed coffee from the State of Nayarita in Northeastern Mexico.…As it cools, an entire orchestra of fruit launches into a complex and juicy counterpoint."

Next, the blended coffees:

Bella Donovan—"The Bella is the wool sweater of our blend—warm, comforting, familiar. Wild and citrusy organic Ethiopian paired with earthy organic Sumatran makes for a vivid and fairly complex Moka/Java blend."

Decaf Noir—"A Swiss water process decaf that is vivid and packed with flavor. Decaf Noir is made from 100 percent organic Swiss water processed decaffeinated beans from East Timor, Sumatra, and New Guinea."

Espresso Temescal—"If we were to commission a sonnet for one of our blends, the Espresso Temescal would be the hands-down choice for this honor. It is complex, poetic, finicky—if you make coffee in your garret, loft studio, pied-à-terre, atelier… this is your blend."

Retrofit Espresso—"Named after the terrorist-proofing of the Bay Bridge BART tube, this espresso is a sweet and simple delight. Not particularly demanding of the barista, the Retrofit is a balanced and mild espresso: the most Italian tasting of any we currently serve."

Roman Espresso—"A bit of a hothouse flower, the Roman Espresso can turn on you in an instant if one of a dozen or so brewing parameters are not to its liking. Generally, it likes lower brewing temperatures, and slower extraction times."

Even though Blue Bottle Coffee is growing, James maintains what he calls "artisan microroasting," which simply means a hands-on process that gets the best from excellent coffee, in a way many consider impractical and time consuming (even fanatical). James will be the first to admit that he's a bit of an obsessed coffee nerd. But in a good way.

He's also particular about the food he serves, as reflected in the carefully crafted menu. Start your day with a bowl of steel cut oats, add brown sugar and whipped butter or seasonal jam and cream—very yum. Maybe you'll take a side of toast with that: Acme Bakery thick toast spread with Larson's Creamery whipped butter and jam from Mountain Fruit Company. How about a brioche? But not just any brioche: this one (accompanied by plum compote and whipped cream) comes from Firebrand Bakery's wood-fired oven.

There's lunch, too—Acme's fresh rolls spread with tasty egg salad or layered with thin slices of handcrafted mortadella or salami from Fra' Mani Salumi in Berkeley. There's probably a little room left for a cookie from the cute girls at Miette's cakes (they have a patisserie in the Ferry Building). James even married one of these cute girls—Caitlin Williams—in 2008.

What does he do when he's not roasting coffee or managing his café and kiosk? James drinks coffee (naturally), goes to the farmer's market, and raises his young son, Dashiell. Sometimes he even pulls out his clarinet. The other day he played *Yellow Submarine* while Dashiell accompanied him on the drums.

"I'm much happier in coffee. It feels like a dream… with the clarinet, I was so close and things never happened the way I wanted them to, and in coffee, every corner we've gone around it's one great thing after another. I feel like I was born to do this," said James. Many coffee connoisseurs think he plays beautiful music.

In 1683, the Turks besieged the city of Vienna. Viennese soldier Franz George Kolshitsky, a Turkish and Arabic speaker, disguised himself as a Turkish soldier, and delivered a plea for help to the nearby Polish troops. The Poles rescued the city, and on September 13, the Turks departed in a hurry, leaving tents, camels, honey, and bags of strange beans (at first thought to be camel feed). Having lived in the Arab world, Kolshitsky knew these were sacks of coffee. He used the reward given him by the mayor for his heroic deed to buy the Turks' coffee and open Central Europe's first coffee house—the Blue Bottle. And that, according to James, is the namesake for his business. You, however, won't have to go through quite as much as Kolshitsky to get your hands on some special coffee. Order James's beans from his website, go to his very cool café at the corner of Jessie and Mint streets next to the Old Mint, or visit his Hayes Street kiosk. There is also a small café in the upscale food court at the Ferry Building and in the Museum of Modern Art. Drink a pot of siphon coffee, a shot of Kyoto-style ice coffee, an espresso, or regular ole' drip coffee. And for the best coffee you'll ever have, try an SG120, a macchiato made with a pure intense shot of single origin coffee from the old, wise, and temperamental Marzocco machine. It's all good here—and James is as particular with his eats as he is with his beans.

NORTH BEACH

*T*his neighborhood still has an Italian flavor——though not as intense as it was at the turn of the twentieth century, when Italian was the language of the street. It remains one of the more interesting areas in the city. Don't even think about nearby Fisherman's Wharf. Come directly here. Walk up to Coit Tower. Visit the Dark Passage house, an art deco apartment building used for exteriors of the 1948 Humphrey Bogart flick by the same name.

Caffè Greco

423 Columbus Avenue
(415) 397-6261
7AM–11PM, Monday to Friday
7AM–midnight, Saturday & Sunday
www.caffegreco.com

*W*hen Caffè Greco opened on August 24, 1988, some folks rolled their eyes and said, "Just what we need—another coffee place in North Beach." But they did. Owners Hanna and Sandra Suleiman have influenced local coffee drinkers from the very beginning, converting them from San Francisco's over-roasted style of espresso to medium-roast illycaffè.

"I remember I was up all night," said Hanna, a tall elegant man. "The next morning my wife came in, and the guys I had trained opened. I went home. We were still living on the peninsula. I drove back up here later, about 3 pm, and the café was packed. The energy and music made me high. It was such a rewarding thing. It just took off from there.

"My wife, Sandra, really played a major role," he continued. "She's a computer analyst… very organized. My vision was there, and she helped it come through. She was extremely supportive."

Coffee has always been part of Hanna's life. He recalls waking up in the morning to his mother roasting coffee on the balcony. "As kids we'd sit and grind it," said Hanna. "My dad

would pour a little coffee in the saucer for me. We drank a lot of Turkish coffee. In Beirut, I grew up drinking Turkish coffee, which is similar to espresso in some ways."

(In case you're not sure how to make Turkish coffee—put finely ground coffee, water, and sugar in a *cezve*, a small Turkish coffee pot. Heat it, then pour the thick, dark, foamy liquid into a *fincan* or coffee cup, and enjoy.)

Time passed and Hanna's interest in coffee continued to percolate. He graduated in pre-med studies from the American University of Beirut—however, he said, "I wanted to be an engineer all my life." So he came to Michigan and got degrees in chemical engineering and business from Wayne State University in Detroit. This was followed by work on the East Coast and then a move to San Francisco, which Hanna said reminded him a lot of Beirut.

Later, while working as a chemical engineer for a German company, and commuting from San Francisco to its Frankfurt and Milan offices, Hanna fell in love with good Italian espresso. In those days, he said, "when you'd drink the espresso there, and then come here, it was just worlds apart.

"In the late 1970s, I was introduced to the illycaffè in Milan, and I was blown away. At the time, the company was growing slowly, although they had been in business for many years. I started to bring illy home because you couldn't get it in the US. As I was traveling extensively, I kept thinking, 'Why can't we have a decent cup of coffee in San Francisco?'" Eventually, he decided to do something about it.

This is a man with a lot of energy—he made plans for a new café in North Beach (the land of the café) while commuting at 30,000 feet to a demanding engineering job in Europe.

Not to mention he'd already opened a gourmet food store, International Gourmet, in San Carlos run by his sister.

Hanna decided to look for a place on Columbus Avenue in San Francisco's North Beach, pinpointing the block between Green and Vallejo streets. At the time, Ben Friedman, a rock poster entrepreneur, owned Greco's current location and the space next door.

Friedman's initial inventory came from famous producer Bill Graham. The always colorful and sometimes cranky Friedman talked Graham into selling him, for peanuts, psychedelic posters from his Avalon and Fillmore West venues. Friedman then turned around and sold the posters for a tidy profit in his legendary Postermat shop at the corner of Vallejo and Columbus streets. At one time, he owned the biggest inventory of rock posters in the world (more than one million)—pallet loads of inventory, which he sold later when he got out of the business for health reasons. If you frequented North Beach in the 1970s and 1980s, you might remember Friedman lurking in the poster shop—Gabby Hayes in a Greek fisherman's cap. He died in 2003 at age 91.

"I worked on Ben for about a year and a half to get this spot. Finally, I struck a deal with him and the concept of Caffè Greco was born," said Hanna. He served illycaffè from day one.

Hanna met Ernesto Illy, the late chairman of illycaffè, in the1980s at a symposium, and they developed a friendship over the years. Both men were scientifically minded, sharing an interest in the quality and chemistry of coffee. "I told Dr. Illy that I wanted to open a place and use his coffee. That's why illycaffè and Caffè Greco became synonymous—we kind of launched illy in the US from here," Hanna said. "He was an amazing individual, all science—and didn't really have much of a business mind. His passion was to promote coffee. He devoted all his life to studying coffee and its complexity."

What complexity, you ask? That cup of espresso you're drinking is derived from 1,550 chemicals—850 volatile and 700 soluble. So to understand it, as Ernesto Illy did, one needs chemistry, physics, math, botany, and lots more. Thanks in part to his efforts, you no longer have to settle for burnt espresso or that stewed swill in the coffee maker.

Ernesto Illy's father, Francesco, a Hungarian chocolate maker and ex-serviceman, settled in Trieste after World War I. The port city handled many of the coffee beans headed to Europe, and in 1933, Francesco started a coffee production and sales company. Ernesto Illy joined the family firm in 1947 after earning a degree in chemistry from the University of Bologna. The coffee baton passed to Ernesto (or Dr. Illy, as he was fondly called) in 1963, when he became chairman of illycaffè.

He focused on selling espresso coffee of consistently high quality through a scientific approach and technical innovation. To do this, Dr. Illy spent much time in the laboratory perfecting equipment that precisely controlled all 100+ steps in the roasting process.

One of these steps involved partnering with Sortex, an English company, to create a sorting machine that analyzes the intensity of light reflected from every bean. As the beans fall into bins, photoelectric cells pinpoint the inferior ones and remove each with a strong puff of air—all of this at warp speed, about 400 beans per second. He claimed it took 50 to 55 beans to make a good cup of espresso, and only one bean to ruin it.

In addition, illycaffè originated a pressurizing technique—inert gas is used to replace oxygen in the can, preserving the coffee's freshness for up to two years. A side benefit: the gas slowly ages the coffee in the can and improves its flavor.

On his quest for the best, Dr. Illy helped growers in Brazil and elsewhere, through education and training, to produce very high-quality arabica beans. "Almost every roaster I know, except for illycaffè, has different grades of coffee, which are normally a combination grown in different regions, with different ratios of arabica and robusto beans," said Hanna. "Dr. Illy earmarked plantations and established relationships with those growers. Illy uses nothing but 100-percent handpicked arabica beans, grown at least 2,000 feet and up. One grade of bean." The *Ambasciatore del Caffè* (his nickname around the world) had a goal for his product: zero defects.

It is said that Dr. Illy helped pioneer the modern concept of branding: make a promise to the consumer and keep it. Illycaffè's promise—a single blend of arabica coffee as close to perfect as humanly possible.

If you experience a large dose of stomach acid and a mega-zap of caffeine after a cup of less-than-perfect drip coffee, here's why: As you pour the boiling water over ground coffee beans in the cone filter (a roughly five-minute process), most of the coffee's water-soluble substances become part of your morning cuppa'. That would be large quantities of caffeine and acid. On the other hand, when drawing an espresso, you get only 60 to 70 percent of the caffeine and half the acid.

Here are your guidelines for making the perfect espresso, according to Dr. Illy. Extract for no more than 30 seconds—in that time, you should draw a small shot (30 milliliters) of liquor-like espresso with dense *crema* (foam) on top. It should flow out of the nozzle into your cup like a rat's tail. Light-colored foam means that either the grind was too

coarse, time too short, or water not hot enough (or all of the above). Very dark *crema* with a hole in the middle signifies an overly fine grind. If you overextract, you'll get white foam with big bubbles.

Another thing to watch for in your quest for the perfect espresso is "channeling." This aberration occurs when you fail to tamp the grounds in the espresso basket with even pressure, or you use a deep basket (say for a double espresso). The water tends to overextract from some spots and underextract from others, channeling narrowly through the grounds. With a single basket, there is less chance of channeling, according to Hanna.

Hanna seconds the 30-second rule: "When you go over 25 to 30 seconds you get into extracting caffeine. The first 15 to 20 seconds you have hardly any caffeine. I could drink 30 cups of coffee with a shorter extraction, and have less caffeine than one regular drip coffee." The Italians refer to a short extraction as a *ristretto* (concentrated or condensed), and Hanna prefers to drink two of these as opposed to a double espresso.

"To me, it is a total science," he

explained. "When you think about it from the scientific point of view, you start to understand what makes a good cup of coffee and a bad cup of coffee. And how a good cup of coffee is not made accidentally."

In light of this information, you may want to polish your barista skills. And illycaffè has just the place. Their Università del Caffè (UDC) in Trieste offers a number of "coffee nerd" courses devoted to understanding coffee and how to make a really good espresso. There are actually 11 UDC international sites, including one in New York.

At Caffè Greco, "nobody gets behind the machine until I train them," says Hanna. His guys (most have been with him since the beginning) know immediately if there is a problem. For example, when the humidity changes, they'll adjust the grinder. More humidity requires a coarser grind so the coffee grains don't stick together."

Water is also important. Hanna checks the water filtration system on his machine every six weeks. "I look at the acidity, check the ph level, and change the

filter. A certain amount of hardness in the water is necessary. Flat water does not make a good cup of coffee. You need calcium and magnesium to bind the molecules together," he explained.

In addition, the commercial espresso machine at Greco is backwashed every night—a process that involves forcing water and special espresso cleaner up into the machine to clean built-up coffee oil and residue from the three-way valve. This valve controls water flowing from boiler to brew head, and brew head to drip tray. It also relieves pressure, so that when removing the portafilter (the basket with coffee grounds), the machine doesn't blow coffee grounds all over the kitchen counter.

First thing in the morning, before opening, Greco baristas make (and throw out) about eight espressos in order to "wake up" the machine. This starts the process of coating the brewing path with fresh coffee, which continues as the day progresses, enhancing the flavor of each espresso. By closing time, you get your best cup.

"Notice something when you have guests," said Hanna. "You make five espressos on your home machine, and the last one is usually the best of all."

You will, however, have a difficult time drawing a consistently good espresso from your home machine. It does not have the pressure/temperature control and ability to stabilize (from running all the time) that its commercial big brother has.

Now that you can talk coffee and espresso machines with the best of them, it's time to check out the eats at Caffè Greco. This is a very good place for something sweet, and as you would expect, Hanna has very high standards.

To begin with, he offers three different cakes made by pastry chef extraordinaire Gary Rulli of Pasticceria Rulli (also profiled in this book)—sacripantina, braziliana, and tartufo. "He still delivers to me because we were one of the first people to patronize him 20 years ago," Hanna said.

The cheesecake is homemade, as are the oatmeal and chocolate chip cookies and the special round Greco cookies. The latter are especially yummy, made from Hanna's mother's recipe in either anise or chocolate orange, using only the best butter and Belgian chocolate.

Biscotti come from the family-run Rosetti's Biscotti House in Clovis, California, and a German pastry chef creates the plum, apple, strawberry, and rhubarb tarts, along with pumpkin pie and apple strudel.

"I could not find consistently good panforte, so it took me about five months, and I developed my own recipe," Hanna explained. "I get hazelnuts from Portland and roast them myself. I get organic almonds and pistachios, and I do a special dried fruit and honey. And I add this twist that no one does in Italy, because of my Greek Mediterranean background. I add figs." (His dad was Lebanese and his mother of Greek descent.)

The name Caffè Greco is a tribute to both Hanna's mother and his favorite café in terms of ambience—the famous Antico Caffè Greco of Rome.

Since 2000, when he sold his interest in the German engineering firm, Hanna has been kicking back—which for him is spending time at his Hawaii home, traveling, keeping Caffè Greco on track, jogging six to eight miles a day, swimming, and, of course, drinking good coffee. "It's my only vice," said Hanna. His son, Sasha, who was nine at the time Caffè Greco opened and more or less grew up there, has become part of the team. He helped with the design of a recent interior facelift for Greco.

So what does a person have to do to get a good coffee in this town? Go to Caffè Greco, where they make your espresso and cappuccino exclusively with illycaffè. For lunch, try one of the focaccia sandwiches, followed by a slice of (really amazing) panforte, made from owner Hanna Suleiman's recipe. It rivals its counterparts from Siena. All the sweets will please, especially the "almost proprietary" Greco cookie—orange flavored, dipped in Belgian chocolate. If you opt for the tiramisu (made from their own recipe), you'll be in good company. Actress Marisa Tomei comes here for it when she's in town. Francis Coppola is also a regular.

Cavalli Café

1441 Stockton Street (at Columbus Avenue)
(415) 421-4219
11AM–11PM, Monday to Saturday
11AM–6:30PM, Sunday
www.cavallicafe.com

*I*n 1872, looking for opportunity and a little adventure, young Giorgio Flavio immigrated to America from Verscio, a small village in Switzerland's Italian-speaking canton of Ticino, just north of Milan. This was not your poor starving Swiss/Italian peasant—the 21-year-old had graduated from a prep school in Locarno and then earned a degree as a civil engineer and surveyor from the University of Geneva.

He landed in the vastly different world of Elko, Nevada, and worked, for a while, in the silver mines. Eventually, he decided to try his luck in San Francisco, where he labored as a waiter, grocery clerk, and musician—and polished his English. After a period as a surveyor in Santa Barbara, this enterprising young man put together enough money to open an Italian language bookstore in North Beach, San Francisco's little Italy. He also Americanized his name, changing it to George Flavius Cavalli.

Cavalli & Co.'s first location was at 32 Montgomery Avenue (renamed Columbus Avenue after the earthquake) from 1880 to 1889. The business flourished and became a focal point for the Italian community. People liked the fact that they could buy books and newspapers from the old country—and, they liked Giorgio himself, who was charming, cultured and well read; yet had his feet firmly planted on the ground. He was friendly to everyone.

Next, the growing establishment moved to a larger space just up the street, at 47 Montgomery Avenue. In addition to selling Italian print media, the *Libreria Italiana* (Italian Bookstore), as the big sign on the building read, offered a notary public service. At this point, Giorgio had been in business for ten years, and although very successful, he had always wanted his own newspaper. The timing was right, and he bought the Swiss/Italian paper, *L'Elvezia*, which he ran until 1904 when he sold it to another Italian-language publication.

Giorgio also wrote two books, *The Book of the Immigrant* and *An English-Italian Grammar*, and, after his first trip back to Europe in 1889, he penned a collection of travel memoirs. One of these describes the half hour he spent in a train car with a group of very green Swiss and Italian immigrants, and relates their desperate, naïve, and hopeful expectations of a new life in California.

It was during the early 1900s that Giorgio brought his younger sister, Angiolina, over from Bellinzona, Switzerland, to help with the bookstore. A few years later, the great earthquake and fire severely damaged the center of San Francisco, including Cavalli & Co.'s premises, and the business moved once again, further up the street to 263 Columbus Avenue. (Coincidentally, this location has been the home of City Lights Booksellers & Publishers since 1953, when poet Lawrence Ferlinghetti opened the doors.)

Cavalli & Co. flourished at that spot for another twelve years until, in 1919, Giorgio moved yet again, to 255 Columbus—now occupied by Vesuvio Café, which was made famous in the beatnik era when it became a hangout for Jack Kerouac, Neal Cassady, and other beat notables.

This expansion turned the *libreria* into an Italian emporium selling a variety of things (mostly Italian), including fountain pens, photographs, Kodak cameras, musical instruments, phonographs, and records. In fact, Cavalli became a major distributor of RCA products in San Francisco.

Giorgio's sister Angiolina married a man named Luigi Giannone, and the couple eventually bought the business from her brother, who by this time had put in 50 years of hard work. The couple's first action was to construct the Cavalli Building, a new and

permanent home for the rechristened A. Cavalli & Co. ("A" for Angiolina), at the corner of Stockton and Columbus.

A year later, in 1935, Giorgio Cavalli died. (His funeral was massive.) And, a year after that, Angiolina and her husband, despondent over the fact that Giorgio was gone, sold the business to journalist Renato Marrazzini, owner and editor of *L'Italia*, San Francisco's daily Italian newspaper and the only Italian paper on the West Coast.

Enter the Valentini family. In the late 1930s, John P. Valentini, a young college grad from St. Mary's began working at A. Cavalli & Co., where he met Marrazzini's stepdaughter. Eventually they married, and in the early 1940s Valentini began managing the store. It didn't hurt that he'd married the boss's daughter; however, his vision for A. Cavalli & Co. was the real reason he was put in charge.

Although still at the center of the North Beach Italian community, the business had fallen somewhat from its peak in the 1920s, and Valentini's drive to make it "the" premier location for book and record signings pushed Cavalli back into the limelight. All the big-name Italians and Italian-Americans stopped here when they came to town.

Over the years, this list included legends Frank Sinatra, Perry Como, and Mario Lanza; famous postwar opera stars such as soprano Renata Tebaldi and tenors Giuseppe di Stefano and Luciano Pavarotti; Italian pop singers Gianni Morandi and Domenico Modugno (of *Volare* fame); author and journalist Luigi Barzini; Enrico Fermi (Nobel Prize winner in physics); and filmmaker Francis Ford Coppola.

The jocks also frequented A. Cavalli & Co., and at the top of the list were heavyweight boxing champ Rocky Marciano and slugger Joe DiMaggio. (The legendary ballplayer for the New York Yankees from 1936 through 1950 was a local boy who'd made good.)

"My father used to play baseball with DiMaggio," explained John J. Valentini (John P.'s son), a friendly, matter-of-fact guy. "They played sandlot baseball here in the neighborhood. This is before he went into the pros. This was in the 1930s. He used to live up here on Filbert. His mother and father lived there. He used to play at North Beach playground.

"After he finished playing professional baseball, DiMaggio lived in the Marina. He had some flats in the Marina, and he used to do his banking here," continued John. "Every time DiMaggio went to the bank next door, he'd come in to say hello to my dad. Used to call him 'Val.' DiMaggio'd come in the store a couple times a month. And all the years my father knew him, do you think he got an autographed baseball? Never. My dad never asked him."

A North Beach landmark, Saints Peter and Paul Roman Catholic Church, played a prominent part in Joe DiMaggio's life. (After the earthquake, the church burned to the ground at its first location on the corner of Filbert and Grant; reconstruction was completed at its present location, next to Washington Square, in 1924.) It was here that DiMaggio married actress Dorothy Arnold, his first wife, on November 19, 1939, and would have married second wife Marilyn Monroe in 1954 had his divorce from wife number one been recognized in the eyes of the church. Thus, contrary to popular belief, the famous couple married at San Francisco's city hall and later returned for a photo op on the steps of Saints Peter and Paul. DiMaggio's funeral took place at the church on March 11, 1999.

John P. Valentini also piped Italian music from the store into the streets during the 1940s, along with some of Il Duce's speeches, which caused local Italiani to gather outside, and FBI to visit inside. "During the Fascist period, a lot of FBI guys came around. Once a week they'd come in, hang around, and watch," said son John J. "My grandfather owned *L'Italia*, the daily newspaper. You can imagine they were watching him pretty close. Checking the articles to make sure they were pro-America."

In 1955, John P. bought the business from Marrazzini, and two years later expanded to include the space next door, formerly Barbessi's Tailor Shop. The basement of the original store became a radio repair department. The upstairs mezzanine, along the wall, was filled with 78-RPM records, and in front, there were four listening booths. (In case you weren't around in the olden days, in the 1950s and 1960s, listening booths were little soundproof compartments in record stores where you could listen to 78, LP, and 45 records before buying them.)

John J. remembers when he began working in the store. "That was 1956. I used to come in Saturdays and after school to help my dad," he said. "When I started school, I didn't know any English. I thought maybe something was wrong with me. My parents, my grandmother... all spoke Italian. There were a lot of Italians here in those days. All the people in the street, all Italians. The Chinese would not go past Broadway. The beatniks came and that started the change."

You probably know some of the beatnik luminaries: writers, poets, and personalities such as Jack Kerouac, Gregory Corso, Allen Ginsberg, Lawrence Ferlinghetti, Neal Cassady, and Ken Kesey (who had a foot in both the beat 1950s and counterculture 1960s). Then, there is that very famous beatnik—Maynard G. Krebs from the CBS television show, *The Many Loves of Dobie Gillis* (1959–63). Played by Bob Denver, Krebs was known for his horrified reaction to the idea of a job. "Work!" he would screech.

Here's your beatnik primer. The term was coined by *San Francisco Chronicle* columnist Herb Caen in 1958, when everything was a "-nik," from Russia's Sputnik (the first artificial satellite) to a peacenik. Some say Allen Ginsberg's 1955 reading of his poem *Howl* at the Six Gallery in San Francisco's Cow Hollow launched the beatnik movement. Originally used by musicians and writers after World War II, the Beat or Beat Generation signified, as Jack Kerouac put it, "a weariness with all the forms, all the conventions of the world." In a few words—burned out, down and out. Mainstream America hijacked this terminology in the late 1950s and applied it to anyone who rejected contemporary society and its materialism, choosing instead an alternative, bohemian lifestyle.

Fletcher Benton, one of the original beatniks and a highly regarded sculptor, known for large-scale geometric pieces in bronze and steel, remembers his days in North Beach when he was a struggling artist.

"I came out here in 1956 and went straight to North Beach because that's where the artists were. I wanted to hang out. This regular group of us had a big table at a bar called the Coffee Gallery. Poets, writers, and painters—ten to fifteen or so of us. They sold only 3.2 beer. No wine, no hard liquor, and no food.

"By late 1959, we were getting young people in the Coffee Gallery. Almost every night, around midnight, they'd come over to our table and tap one of us on the shoulder, and ask pretty much the same two questions. The first one was, 'Excuse me, have you seen Jack Kerouac?' I'd say no I haven't seen Jack Kerouac.

"And the second question was, 'Do you know of any inexpensive apartments to rent?' We did not want those people there—they were scrubbed behind the ears college students. Very young and naïve," continued Fletcher. "I was paying, at that time, $34 a month and sharing a bathroom.

"We all decided we'd tell them that there is nothing in North Beach because it's a very small area and the Italians own most of the stuff. But there are some Victorian railroad flats (long and narrow with one hallway connecting a single line of rooms) out in the Haight-Ashbury. So they'd go out there—at the time there was nothing going on in the Haight," explained Fletcher. That's why, according to him, there was a population of young people living in the Haight-Ashbury poised to embrace the Summer of Love and the hippies.

After high school, John J. joined the army and then came to work in the store full time. In those days, full time meant exactly that: Monday through Saturday from 9 am to 9 pm. Sunday was the easy day (sort of)—only 9:30 am to 2 pm.

In the late 1970s, two momentous events took place. A four-alarm fire seriously damaged the Cavalli building—the store closed for many months before reopening (as more of a bookstore) in half its former space. The other half became an Italian clothing and tailor shop, owned by Giuseppe Festinese and his brother Toni. This was 1978. Sadly, the following year, after 50 years at A. Cavalli & Co., John P. Valentini passed away. John J. carried on with the family business for the next 27 years.

Around 1998, current owner Santo Esposito began to hang out in the bookstore, along with other young Italians in the area. "I was working as a waiter. I was here every day, between lunch and dinner. It was nice to talk to John about soccer and stuff like that. It was relaxing," said Santo.

As he approached his 50-year anniversary in the family shop, John J. considered retiring—but what to do with the business? There was no family member to step in and take over this cultural and historical landmark. He didn't want to sell to just anybody.

"I always liked the building and the feeling here. That's why I was thinking, when John said maybe he wants to sell… that maybe it could be mine," said Santo. "I asked him if he thought you could mix the bookstore with a café. John said, 'Sure, the landlords are nice. Just talk to them.'"

Roughly a year after John J. and Santo began their discussion about the sale of the business, they sealed the deal. Santo became the new owner on June 30, 2006. "I knew Santo, and he seemed like the right guy," John J. explained. "I wanted to keep it going. It's the only thing left around here."

Santo's life has followed a circuitous route to San Francisco from Ascea Marina, the small, pretty seaside village where he was born and raised. It's located about 50 miles (80 km) south of La Costa Amalfitana and Salerno. "In our house there was a wood-burning pizza oven. We used it every day to make bread, pizza, and biscotti," said Santo, who has three brothers and two sisters. "I grew up like that. And I like working with flour. So eventually I went to work for my friend in Milan for a couple years—he owned a huge pizza place with two wood-burning ovens."

From there, he moved on to Germany and then England as a pizza chef. In 1992, while in London, a friend set up a job for Santo in Houston, Texas; however, when he arrived, the job tuned out to be bogus—the restaurant was shuttered. And Santo was out in the street, literally, with his suitcase. "I didn't know where to go," Santo explains. "I started moving around—in one week, London to Houston, Houston to Dallas... Dallas, LA. In LA, an Italian guy from Milan said go to San Francisco, that's a good place to start."

After a few months in the City by the Bay, Santo returned to London, where he worked once again as a pizza chef, and put some money together before coming back to North Beach in 1998.

Santo's vision of reborn Cavalli Café required some serious renovations—along with hard physical labor on his part. During its transition, the business stayed open while Santo built out the bar, put in a kitchen, lowered the counter, laid a new floor, and opened the mezzanine—all the while keeping the original floor plan. Luckily, his dad worked in construction, so Santo knew how to do everything himself.

"I never saw anyone work like that. Did it all himself," said John J., who helped out during the first three months of the change over.

"Little by little, it changed. Everyday the counter was in a different place. People would grab stuff and try to pay, but they couldn't find the till because it was always moving around. It took a year," adds Santo, an intense, charming, sometimes temperamental, and (obviously) energetic man.

On October 6, 2007, he served his first cappuccino, made with Danesi coffee, a good Italian medium roast. Santo knows how to make a coffee, so when you order an espresso, you get a small shot of syrupy coffee, just like in Italy—same thing with a cappuccino: shot of espresso and a little steamed (not scalded) milk with smooth foam.

Santo learned the basics of espresso making as a 10-year-old, helping out in a bar. Oddly enough, he polished his skills in the Italian Air Force, during three months of punishment duty drawing espresso and cappuccino for the officers.

He makes the coffee he likes, not the coffee he thinks people will like. "I make everything the way I like," Santo said. One thing you can be sure of with Santo's cooking, if he likes it, you'll like it. The menu is filled with what he describes as "tasty Italian home cooking."

"I cook the way I learned at home combined with what I learned working next to Italian chefs. The menu is classic. But I'll make what you want. If you want an omelet, I'll make an omelet. I have regulars who eat here every day. Yesterday, one of them wanted spaghetti, garlic, olive oil, and chili flakes. I cook different things every day, in addition to the specials," he continued.

Then there are the panini—two simple and tasty standouts: speck (smoky-flavored northern Italian prosciutto) and provolone; imported Italian tuna in olive oil, tomato, and

(depending on how Santo feels) basil or chopped black olives.

He makes his own tiramisu—a ubiquitous (and frequently insipid) dolce—however, Santo's version will not disappoint. It seems to float above the plate, a spongy, coffee, rum, and creamy delight; powdered with dark cocoa. If chocolate is your thing, go for the chocolate mousse—again, common and often ordinary—but here, light yet substantial with mini-chunks of chocolate. Also, put Santo's *panna cotta* (cooked cream), a smooth vanilla custard, on your list.

Santo's 17-hour days have eased up a bit—he now has someone who helps with the cooking, and someone else takes care of the cleaning. Plus, his wife, Yanessa, comes to lend a hand for a few hours in the afternoon, while his son, Santo, Jr., and baby girl, Cirila, nap downstairs in the basement of the café. Sometimes, Santo joins them.

No matter how well Santo prepares his food, the addition of a café to Cavalli is troubling to some customers. Many of these are old timers, such as the 92-year-old woman who worked here when she was young. They ask, "Why the change?" In a word: survival.

As John J. said, "We had lots of competition. Amazon, and all the rest." Hopefully, with its new direction, Cavalli Café will continue to be around for many more decades.

Maybe you knew A. Cavalli & Co. when it was a bookstore. Or maybe not. Either way, this new, improved Cavalli Café carries on a tradition that began in 1880. The Valentini family, who ran the place for almost 70 years, has passed the baton to new owner Santo Esposito. He's created a relaxed space with free wi-fi and really good coffee—like they make in Italy, where an espresso is a thick syrupy shot, not a small cup of watery brown liquid, as you get in many places here. His menu is classic, light home cooking. The tiramisu is tops; so is the tuna panino. If you don't see something you like, and it's a dish that Santo could whip up easily in the kitchen, he'll make it for you. Tourists and regulars come here—as does Lawrence Furlinghetti, beat poet, publisher, and owner of City Lights bookstore, who respectfully regales Santo with Cavalli stories from the old days. Another recent visitor: James Gandolfini, of The Sopranos *fame. It's open until 11 PM, so you don't have to endure a late night snack of junk food.*

Caffè Baonecci

516 Green Street
(415) 989-1806
10:30AM–9:30PM, Tuesday to Saturday
12PM–4:30PM, Sunday lunch only
Closed Monday
www.caffebaonecci.com

Danilo Bakery was a North Beach establishment for more than 100 years. Its ovens survived the 1906 earthquake, and some say they're the oldest functioning bakery ovens in the United States.

A few years ago, Signora Danila Di Piramo, who had owned the bakery since 1969 with her brother (and baker) Danilo Di Piramo, wheelchair bound due to an accident, was looking to retire, and preferred selling to an Italian. However, it seemed that no *ragazzi Italiani* were interested in this type of work anymore. Then, she met Walter Gambaccini, a *parrucchiere* (hairdresser) who lived in Altopascio, about 21 kilometers (12 miles) from Lucca and considered Lucca *fuori*. Lucca is divided into *dentro* and *fuori le mura* (inside and outside the wall)—the wall being the protective Renaissance-era fortress circling the old city.

"I've been coming here since 1995, and I met Signora Danila in 2000," explained Walter. He first toured the United States on a solo vacation. Back home, he told his wife that he was *affascinato* (charmed) by the place. In 1996, he brought his wife Stefania (who worked as a tattoo artist), and two sons, Elia and Fillipo, for a visit. The family returned every year and

visited many parts of the country including New York, California, and Nevada—always with a stop in San Francisco for two or three days to visit friends.

"I began looking for a way to live and work here," said Walter. "However, at the time, in the mid-1990s, I had a situation in Italy that was very good for me. *Stavo bene economicamente* (I was doing well economically)."

Walter started as a hairdresser at age 14, working after school for a friend of the family who coifed his mom's hair. He liked the work so he decided to make it a career. Walter did well, and at one point had three partners, twenty employees, and a big shop in Lucca. "The really good times were from 1982 to 1992. We worked a lot and made a lot of money. From there, things started to slow down, and then with the euro, things got more difficult in Italy," said Walter.

La dolce vita (the sweet life) reached its peak with the *sorpasso* in 1987, when Italy announced that its GDP had surpassed that of the UK. Since then, *la dolce vita* has been increasingly less *dolce,* and in many ways became downright sour after the introduction of the euro in January 2002. The cost of living for many Italians rose sharply: for example, during the switchover, some restaurant and bar owners, along with tradesmen, exploited the situation, converting prices at 1,000 lire per euro instead of 1,900 lire.

Some say that Italy's economic problems were inevitable, while others claim they are solely the fault of the euro. In any case, the introduction of the euro forced Italy to change its economic model: out with the survival tactic of high budget deficits, high inflation, and devalued currency; in with low budgets, low inflation, and a single European currency. The resulting adjustment continues to be painful.

"From 2000 to 2002, the *sistema fiscale* grew worse in Italy. There is the now *ricca ricca* (the very rich), the middle class—which is disappearing—and the poor. As the poor class grew, less money was spent on goods and services, such as the hairdresser, and this pushed me to think seriously about my next step," said Walter. In 2003, he began to think about buying a business in the US, and considered a hairdressing salon, but decided against it because his professional qualifications were not recognized, and American clients had different expectations.

Walter then looked at the food business: a pizzeria, restaurant, or an Italian bar—and remembered an early conversation with Signora Danila. She wanted to sell to an Italian in order to continue the tradition of a pasticceria Italiana. (During his American vacation, he usually stopped by to say hello and buy some bread.) "I called from Italy and said, 'Do you remember me?' And she said yes," Walter explained. "I said I'm interested in buying the business."

The deal went through—and Walter and his family took over Danilo Bakery in July 2006. They got an E-2 category visa for foreigners who invest capital in an operating business.

If certain conditions are met (such as paying taxes, remaining self sufficient, etc.), the visa is renewable every five years. Eventually, this opens the door to a green card.

What do hairdressing and baking have in common, you ask? Nothing, unless you're a hairdresser who enjoys baking like Walter, and you come from Altopascio, so renowned for its bread making that it's called *la città del pane* (the city of bread). Walter said, "As a hobby, at home, I had two ovens inside, and one outside for making pizza and foccacia. A couple times a week I'd have a bunch of friends (20 to 40) over and cook for them. So I knew how to make these things, but I was not a pasticciere or panettiere. Two years before we came here, my oldest son, Elia, started working in a *panificio* (bread shop) owned by a friend in Italy. He learned how to make bread. When we arrived, we had to hit the ground running."

By the end of Signora Danila's reign, her bakery looked a bit tired and dingy. Little by little, Walter and family spruced up the interior, painting it bright colors, opening it up and adding seats and tables (including a couple outside)—generally transforming the look and feel.

While the appearance had declined, the quality of Signora Danila's bread and pastry had not. Walter's intent was to improve on this high quality, which he has done successfully. Signora Danila's signature *pane integrale* (whole wheat bread) and *pane di granturco* (cornbread) are now lighter and tastier. The ubiquitous North Beach raspberry ring and cheese Danish have been banished. "We're concentrating on Italian-style brioche. We have three classics like you find in Italy: plain, *crema* (a favorite with Italian customers), and *cioccolata*. Only these three, because I wanted to be different from all the others," explained Walter.

He saw that many of the Italian cafés and bakeries in the area served up a *cucina* (cuisine) from 60 or 70 years ago, when Italian immigrants first opened them. Things in Italy have changed a lot in that period of time, and since he and his family are recent arrivals from *la bell'Italia,* they could, in a sense, offer an Italia *piu vicina*. This includes homemade sweets such as *baci di dama* or lady kisses (round chocolate balls filled with *crema*), *sabbiosini* (the same as *baci di dama*, only without the chocolate), and *cantucci* (what you call biscotti).

The family has freshened up the breakfast menu (served midmorning) by offering a selection of three-egg omelets, such as the uncomplicated *buon giorno e tre uova* (salt, coarse

black pepper, and parsley) or the tasty *Italiana* (tomatoes, basil, black olives, and fresh mozzarella), both served with polenta and your choice of either bread or toasted focaccia. In addition, there is, of course, the traditional cappuccino and brioche (made from the recipe of a friend and pasticciere [pastrymaker] in Lucca).

Lunch and dinner feature Stefania's smooth and hearty *zuppa di farro* (faro soup), made from a *ricetta antica Toscana* (old Tuscan recipe) with tomatoes, garlic, onion, pancetta, and farro. The latter is a grain that looks and tastes like brown rice, although nuttier and sweeter. You have to soak farro before cooking it, and in the pot it stays chewy like Arborio rice. Some also compare farro to spelt, a firm wheat-like grain.

You may feel like a Roman legionnaire when you eat this soup—farro was the standard ration for the empire's soldiers. They ate it in the form of a cooked paste as they busied

themselves with conquering the world. It is believed that farro was also used as currency during the height of the Roman Empire. The Romans, however, were not the first farro aficionados—it was widely consumed in the Middle East and North Africa, and farro grains have been found in ancient Egyptian tombs. Most of Italy's farro is grown in the mountainous Garfagnana region northwest of Lucca, where the grain thrives in a high, barren terrain.

Farro's cultivation dwindled after the fall of the Roman Empire, when higher yielding grains began to replace it, and by the late 1900s, it almost disappeared. Lately, farro has staged a comeback as foodies and good cooks discover its benefits—high fiber, low gluten, and an alphabet of vitamins starting with A, B, and C.

The menu also includes a lovely cracker-thin pizza made from Stefania's recipe, plus an assortment of *focaccine ripiene* (thin, tender, and crusty Lucca-style flatbread sandwiches), including *focaccina con tonno* (tuna, fresh tomatoes, capers, and mayonnaise) and *focaccina vegeteriana* (fresh tomatoes, green salad, mascarpone cheese, and mayonnaise). "Focaccina is characteristic of Lucca, and the towns around it: Versiglia, Viareggio, and Forte dei Marmi," said Walter.

And if you like *fagioli* (beans), this is the place—the Toscani make the best bean dishes in Italy. Stefania's *fagioli all'uccelletto*, cannellini beans in a lightly spiced tomato sauce, defines simple and tasty.

The coffee is good here, too. When you order a shot of espresso, it's drawn as it should be—short with a nice crema. And your cappuccino doesn't come with scalded milk. (They use a coffee called Miscela d'Oro, made by a family-run coffee roaster in Messina, Sicily.) According to Walter, making a good espresso, or *caffè* as the Italians call it, is not brain surgery. It simply takes a little care. Use a good machine and quality coffee. Get to know the machine—each has its own personality—and then adjust for the weather. If it's sunny, grind the beans finer; and if it's cold and rainy, grind less fine because the beans will swell up.

When Walter and family bought Danilo Bakery, they changed the name to Caffè Baonecci. The reason: "We wanted to add our own touch. In Lucca, when something is *bella* or *buona*, you say *bao necci,* as in, *"Ti piace questo cappuccino—è buono?"* (Do you like this cappuccino—is it good?) And you answer, *"E' buono bao necci."* Or there's *"una ragazza bao necci,"* said Walter. *"A Lucca, abbiamo sempre in bocca queste parole* (In Lucca, we always use this phrase). In nearby Viareggio, they don't use *bao necci.* It's just part of the dialect in Lucca."

At Caffè Baonecci, you'll be served by the Gambaccini family, fresh from Lucca. There's charming Walter, his wife Stefania with the striking aquamarine eyes, and their two handsome sons Elia and Filippo. Come for a late breakfast (a genuine brioche and cappuccino like you get in Italy). At lunchtime or dinner, try a tasty thin crust pizza or focaccina ripiena (flat bread sandwich filled with tuna and prosciutto, or mascarpone and tomatoes). They also sell imported Italian sundries such as coffee and pasta. This is a nice place to hang out—with Italians, North Beach locals, tourists, and even the Chinese, who have begun to discover it. In fact, you never know who'll turn up. Once Italian actress Cinzia Mascoli stumbled on Baonecci. She is best known for her role as Valeriana in the Carlo Verdone film Viaggi e Nozze (1995). Comedian Bill Cosby has also paid Baonecci a visit. Drop by on Thursday evenings for pizza and a classic Italian movie, shown on the big 65-inch flat screen TV.

Liguria Bakery

1700 Stockton Street (at Filbert)
(415) 421-3786
8AM–2PM, **Monday to Friday**
7AM–2PM, **Saturday**
7AM–noon, **Sunday**

*B*efore the great earthquake and fire of April 18, 1906, St. Peter's Episcopal Church stood at the corner of Stockton and Filbert streets, across from Washington Square Park. Afterward, the edifice was completely destroyed, and the park became a tent city for 600 homeless San Franciscans. Those who still had a home set up temporary cooking stoves outside in the front yard or at the curb. It was assumed that all chimneys were damaged, and no fires were permitted in interior fireplaces, grates, or stoves by order of Hizzoner, Mayor E. E. Schmitz.

During the process of rebuilding homes and businesses in post-tumbler San Francisco, the city fathers decided to remedy the street name confusion that had resulted in many letters being delivered to the wrong address. There were numerous streets with identical names (such as Church Street and Church Avenue), along with three different sets of numerical streets/avenues, and streets that changed names frequently within a few blocks.

In spring of 1909, part of this cleanup included changing the name of Montgomery Avenue to Columbus Avenue. Laid out in the mid 1800s, Montgomery Avenue branched off Montgomery Street and ran on an angle to the bay, clipping off a corner of Washington Square at Union Street, which created the small triangular extension of the park you see today.

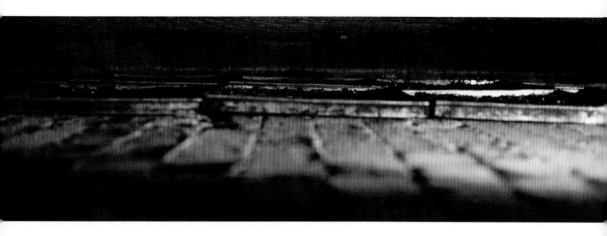

About this time, Ambrosio Soracco emigrated from the Genoa area of Liguria (comune of Chiavari) and worked in bakeries on Union Street and Grant Avenue. He was one of the many Genovesi who came to San Francisco in the 1880s through the early 1900s. Entrepreneurial and tight with a buck, they tended to dominate life among the Italian migrants of North Beach, which also included Lucchesi, Siciliani, and Calabresi.

By 1911, Ambrosio decided to open his own place, Liguria Bakery, in the building constructed at the former site of the ravaged St. Peter's Episcopal Church. Roughly a year later, with the bakery up and running, he sent for his brothers, Giuseppe and Giovanni.

The Soraccos baked sourdough bread, panettone, and hardtack for the North Beach Italians, making home deliveries by horse and wagon. Their business flourished until 1938 when Ambrosio died suddenly, when he was only in his early 50s. His two brothers left shortly afterward and settled in Napa, on a ranch near Soda Springs, growing olives, drying mushrooms, and making wine—all of which they sold in North Beach. Neither man ever married.

In the meantime, Ambrosio's widow, Mary, kept the bakery running until her 10-year-old son, George, became old enough to take over. "My dad started after he graduated from high school, and he's been working there all this time," said George's son, Michael Soracco. He runs Liguria along with his siblings Danny and Mary, their mother Josephine, and George, who still comes into work. The family owns the business, but over the years has had a collection of partners.

Liguria's focus on focaccia (an Italian flatbread) came about in the early 1950s when the large bakeries such as Parisian tried to dominate the market. "They would go into the stores where the old timers were established," explained Michael. "And say, 'If you buy bread from us, we'll give you a month free and only charge you a nickel a loaf.'

"Then the store mangers would ask guys like my dad, 'What are you going to give us?'

"They'd answer, 'We're just going to keep giving you good bread like always.'

"Before these old timers would give anything away, they were going to leave the flour in the sacks. That's when we stopped making bread and started making focaccia, which nobody else had. I was born in 1956. And I can't remember them making bread, ever," said Michael. For a while, Liguria also made panettone and biscotti, but discontinued that around 1984, as the neighborhood began to lose more and more of its Italian flavor, and demand for these products diminished.

Michael has been in the business since 1981. That's a lot of focaccia. His workday begins at 3AM. In fact, he often crosses Broadway Street on his way to the bakery when the party animals are just winding down. "I mix the dough right when I come in. Takes about an hour. Everything is fresh. By 5AM my brother comes in, and my mom and sister come in at 7 or 7:30. My dad also comes in early," he said. His workday ends when many people are just getting to the office—9AM. One or two deliveries, and he's home by 11 am. Bedtime is 8 or 9PM.

On slow days, Michael makes 200 pounds of focaccia dough in a huge mixer that holds water and 280 pounds of flour. On weekends, the busiest period, it's close to 500 pounds day. The brisk walk-in trade has slowed considerably since 9/11—now, most of the sales are commercial. "We're lucky. We don't have to pay employees. We're all family. My dad owns the building with some cousins so the rent is very reasonable. We can survive these turbulent times," explained Michael.

That being said, you better come in the morning if you want any of this great focaccia, because by noon it's often sold out. There are the four original old-stand-by flavors: plain, raisin, green onion, and tomato sauce/onion. If you're not a purist, try the newer list composed of garlic, olive, mushroom, rosemary, and rosemary/garlic. This focaccia is superb: light and delicate with a slightly sweet finish.

"My grandfather came up with the recipe," said Michael. "We do everything the same. We use the freshest, best quality ingredients, and don't cut any corners." The recipe for the dough, however, remains a tightly held family secret (you won't get access, even with a high-level security clearance).

Once the dough rises, Michael stretches it onto huge metal trays, pokes the little dimples on top (using a special roller with fingers), then adds the topping, and bakes the focaccia at a very high temperature for 8 to 10 minutes. The large, 30-feet-deep, brick oven is original, constructed with the building and modified very little in the past 100 years—the Soracco family changed it from wood-burning to gas and replaced the inside bottom level of bricks. A big, evil-looking gas blower, hanging outside the oven, heats the interior by shooting a flame inside from 8:30 to 11AM every morning. The interior reaches 800 degrees, incinerating any focaccia residue. The oven door is then closed, and the next morning, when it's time to bake, the temperature is perfect. The oven must be heated everyday, because if the bricks cool down, they will crumble.

As a kid, growing up in North Beach, Michael lived within a two-block radius of the bakery. He said, "It was basically all Italians in the neighborhood here. We knew everybody who came in the store. They'd line up Sunday morning after mass at Saints Peter and Paul. And if they didn't leave mass early, they wouldn't get in."

"We never stayed home. I spent a lot of my time at the Salesian Boys' Club. We played football, basketball, and baseball. During summer it was open from ten to noon, then you'd break for lunch, and go back from one to five. Break for dinner, and after, it was open from seven to nine. It was two dollars a year to join," continued Michael.

In 1859, Italian priest Don Bosco started a society of priests, brothers, and nuns with a mission to "roll up their sleeves" and work with the poor children of Torino. He adopted St. Francis de Sales as his patron; thus, his society became known as the Salesians.

The Salesians (or Society of St. Francis de Sales) exported their good works to the United States, and in 1918, Father Oreste Trincheri started the Salesian Boys' Club next to Sts. Peter and Paul Church. The idea was to keep the North Beach *ragazzi* (boys) off the streets and help them channel their creative energy in the positive direction of sports, dramatics, and music. In 1994, this very successful organization opened its doors to girls, and renamed itself the Salesian Boys' and Girls' Club.

Michael's boyhood world also included Saturday matinees at the Palace, the North Beach neighborhood theater and art deco gem (with a graceful, winding interior staircase) that showed double features such as *Desperate Journey* (1942) with Errol Flynn and Ronald Reagan, and *Sin Town* (1942) starring Broderick Crawford. Originally, it was called the Washington Square Theater, a venue for live performance, including operas featuring Enrico Caruso. Sadly, the Palace has ended its life as the refurbished (and now boarded-up) Pagoda Palace.

Stand in Washington Square, look around its periphery, and imagine the neighborhood of Michael's youth. Italian was the first language of the street. A Rexall Drugstore stood on the corner of Union and Columbus—the present location of Coit Liquor, which was originally two doors down. You would have purchased your new dinette set at Figoni Furniture (since morphed into Moose's Restaurant and then Joey & Eddie's Italian Restaurant) next door to the post office. The hat store in the same block was a Modern Cleaners.

And of course, there was Liguria Bakery, where it has always been for almost 100 years.

"I knew if I didn't do the business, then that would be it," says Michael. "You could sell it, but it would never be the same. So far it has worked out fine. It is a decent living, but we work seven days a week."

But, he points out, it was worse in the old days. "They started at 6 and didn't get home until 6 at night. They were there a good 12 hours every day. They baked, delivered, and sold."

The following is a story told by Michael's dad, George (a man of few words), about the old days. It illustrates how a long day can end up feeling a lot longer. "They used to do the home deliveries," said Michael. "They'd go in these flats or apartments, and some of them had four or five floors. A family would say, 'We want one bread a day.' And my dad would be doing the deliveries, so he'd walk up all these stairs. All of a sudden, he'd get to the top of the fifth stairway, and there would be a note: 'Don't need bread today.'"

Now, most customers come to them—including Francis Coppola, who has been a regular for a long time. Also, celebrity chef and generally over-the-top personality Mario Batali came in to film a segment for his show *Molto Mario* on the Food Network. "He made focaccia back in the kitchen. We gave him the dough and then he put it in the oven and took it out with the paddle. He's pretty knowledgeable about all the stuff we do," said Michael. (Mario now finishes his pizzas by drizzling olive oil over the topping just before baking, a trick he learned from Liguria.)

There's a lot of focaccia floating around out there, but no one makes it like the Soracco family at Liguria Bakery. And they've been doing it a long time—way before it was ubiquitous and chic. The big scale inside this plain storefront still works, but they don't weigh your focaccia anymore. Each big slab comes wrapped in white paper like the old days. Classic flavors are still the best: plain, raisin, green onion, and tomato sauce/ onion. The old phone number with the exchange name, Garfield 13786 (not much different than the current 421-3786), is still on the window. Michael Soracco, his siblings Danny and Mary, and their mom, Josephine, run the business. Get there early in the day—before noon—or you're likely to find only a few crumbs left on the shelf. Liguria closes during the month of August and between Christmas Eve and New Year's Eve.

· 3 ·

SUNSET DISTRICT & VICINITY

*T*he area was once all sand dunes. Now it's a cluster of neighborhoods bordering on Golden Gate Park and its panhandle. Visit Alamo Square near the tip of the panhandle on the cusp of the Haight, and see a spectacular view of the city, along with the famous row of Painted Ladies. Next hit the Inner Sunset at 9th and Irving just off the park, and then ride the N Judah streetcar to the end of the line at Ocean Beach, where San Francisco ends and 7,400 miles of Pacific Ocean—all the way to Sydney, Australia—begin.

Java Beach Café

Near Golden Gate Park
1396 La Playa Street
  (at Great Highway)
(415) 665-5282
5:30AM–11PM, Monday to Friday
6AM–11PM, Saturday & Sunday

At the San Francisco Zoo
2650 Sloat Boulevard (at 45th Avenue)
(415) 731-2965
5:30AM–11PM, Monday to Friday
6AM–11PM, Saturday & Sunday
www.javabeachcafe.com

When Pat Maguire stopped drinking and hanging out in bars, he started frequenting cafés. And, after a while, he began to wonder why there wasn't one in his Ocean Beach neighborhood, at the end of Judah Street where it meets the Great Highway (and the great Pacific Ocean). This was the late 1980s, before the Starbucks invasion.

Pat explained: "I'd go up to these coffee house owners and say, 'Hey, in the Outer Sunset there are no cafés. You should open one up.'

"They'd go, 'Yeah, but there's not much going on out there.'

"And I'd say, 'Well there would be if you opened a café.' And so I went from place to place, and the same thing. Then one day it dawned on me, why don't I do it, even though I don't know what I'm doing." Pat had been working as a union carpenter.

After looking around, he decided on his current location, inhabited at the time by a boarded-up (and infamous) bar called Dicks at the Beach. "I was sitting on those stairs by

the beach at the end of Judah Street, and I looked across at this gutted, beat-up building. Suddenly, in my mind's eye, I saw what's here today," said Pat.

This was in spite of the fact that everyone from the neighborhood knew you didn't hang out at Judah and the Great Highway. It was rough (but not dangerous), especially at night when the Animals, the nickname for a hard-drinking group of hobos and local Sunset boys, caroused in the tunnel leading to the beach. This group actually had a code: don't mess with the neighborhood. "Being as I had been one of those guys, who had hung out down here, I knew the area," Pat said.

He decided to approach the building's owner, who lived in an apartment above the bar. "Since I never went to college and didn't know a lot about business, I asked a friend what businessmen wear. He said they wear a suit and carry a briefcase. So I got this briefcase, and put on a suit. I didn't want to look like a neighborhood guy," recalled Pat.

"I got to the door, and was about to ring the doorbell when fear stuck me. I said to myself, 'What am I doing? I'm out here in a suit on Judah and the Great Highway.' I go, 'This is stupid, man.' I took three steps to walk away, and something stopped me. I just turned around and said what the heck. And bing-bong, rang the doorbell. I was 24 years old."

Even though the owner had planned to convert Dicks at the Beach to an apartment the following week, he agreed to give Pat's café a shot.

Pat said, "Thank god, he didn't ask me for a pen, or anything. There was nothing in the briefcase. He and I became quite friendly with each other over the years. The serendipity of it was that Java Beach almost didn't happen. But it did and changed everything. Not only for this neighborhood, but also for my life.

"My first day, we opened at 7AM and there was an entire women's soccer team waiting outside. There were people all over, with balloons. I think before I even opened my doors there were close to 40 people standing out here. I almost had a heart attack. I said, 'Oh no.' I didn't say, 'Oh yeah.' It was, 'Oh no.' I was still learning how to make an espresso and a cappuccino. I thought I was going to have time. People just swarmed us. And we were still trying to figure out how to work the register. They were nice, saying, 'You guys'll get it. Don't worry about it.'"

At noon, Pat's family came to help, while he ran up the street to a former café/hang out and poached a barista he knew. "I said, 'How much are they paying you?' And she said, 'Six bucks an hour.' I go, 'I'll pay you nine,'" explained Pat. She showed up at 3PM after work and was his first employee.

Pat had a business partner for a short while, but early on, he said, "This is too much," and left. "There was no going out or to parties anymore. It was just work. I'd open in the morning. I'd close at night, and I mopped the bathrooms. My only break would be to go shopping. We didn't have any deliveries, so I'd drive down to Costco. This thing had taken my whole life over," said Pat.

One of the Java Beach blessings is that Pat's future wife, Buffy, came sauntering in one day. She was on her summer break from Smith College. Eventually, they started to date—sort of. "I'd say, 'You can hang out, but I can't go anywhere. My partner just disappeared, so I'm the guy,'" said Pat.

So she started to help out, and freshen Pat's décor, which consisted of worn coffee tables and bookcases, along with old couches he'd found on the street. He recalls, "One guy came in and said, 'Hey, that's my couch! I'm glad someone's getting some use out of it.'"

Buffy also brought a business savvy that Pat didn't have. Her half-Irish, half-Sicilian family of bar and restaurant owners ran businesses in North Beach and on the Embarcadero. Buffy added the food and beverage knowhow, while Pat provided the neighborhood face—the guy that everybody knew. "There was also my work ethic," he added. "Just being able to put in hours and not give up."

Pat's perseverance was put to the test when, later on, he had the opportunity to buy the Java Beach building. His lease had run out, and he thought, "If I don't get this building now, I could be bumped out and lose everything I've built." In the middle of negotiations with the owner, Pat learned that someone had outbid him by $100,000. Suddenly, the sale was up in the air.

"That broke my heart," said Pat. "I was struggling to come up with the money. How am I going to do it, now? I was in extreme fear. I was going, how can this be? I think I'm blessed. And now this happens. It sent me into a state of confusion... and almost darkness."

His sister-in-law, Maureen, suggested a nine-day novena to St. Joseph. "I thought anything is worth a try. These are the type of things you do when you're desperate," Pat explained. He was leaving for Jerusalem to attend the wedding of Buffy's best friend—what better place to ask the Lord for a favor.

Every morning, he went from his hotel in the Old City to the Church of the Holy Sepulcher and prayed at the foot of the cross: "God, please, please don't let them take this place from me. Please, Lord, you know how hard I've worked."

On the eighth day, he had a revelation: "What am I doing? Coming here like this. I'm trying to be a manipulator of God—a bad lawyer in God's presence. So I said, 'God, I just want to say I'm sorry for the way I've been. Matter of fact, I have a new prayer—It's in your hands.'

"And I had this peace... this unbelievable peace," added Pat. He told his wife Buffy, and then called his mom, Christy, to relay his new attitude toward the sale of the building. She said they were filming a movie at Ocean Beach, and that there was a photo in the *San Francisco Examiner* of the actors in front of Java Beach. "What's the movie called?" Pat asked.

She answered, "*In God's Hands*." (A 1998 surf movie about big wave riders.)

And so, he got the message a second time—and, in the end, got the building, too.

Pat describes his mom as someone who quietly "walked the walk" her entire life. She not only raised her young family of five boys and two girls after her husband, John, a mechanical engineer for Southern Pacific Railroad, passed away at age 52, but, over the years, took in 8

or 10 kids off the street. "One kid was homeless and living in Stern Grove," said Pat. "When she found out, she said, 'Go get that guy.'"This 14-year-old's name was Pat Lawlor, who later became a boxer and fought in a number of middleweight title bouts. All the Maguire boys were boxers, and Pat's younger brother Danny, a light heavyweight, turned professional, but was forced to retire after seven wins and one loss, due to eye damage.

Another "adopted" stray was a kid Pat hired to work in the café. "A young hood… out of some halfway house. I not only gave him a job, but brought him to my mom and said, 'This guy doesn't have a home, ma,'" explained Pat.

"She goes, 'Show him where the beds are.'" He grew up at the Maguire house, and now is a respected policeman and undercover cop.

During Christy's funeral in September 2007, there was quite a family procession—her sons were pallbearers, with all the guys who grew up in her house following the coffin.

Pat continues to follow his mom's philosophy at Java Beach: Don't bother people. Don't terrorize people with your beliefs. Instead, live a good life.

The people who come to Java Beach include local surfers and board riders from Marin and the peninsula. In fact, it was a big wave, long-board surfer and surf artist named Llewellyn Ludlow III who created the sign on the front of the Java Beach building. Pat said, "I told him I needed a sign, but I didn't have any money, so how about this, 'You paint me that sign, and you never buy a thing here, ever.'

"He said, 'Yeah, I like that deal, nice.' He's a funny guy, a big blond-headed surfer. Sixteen years, he is still getting his free sandwich."

Llewelyn Ludlow III also painted the sign for the second Java Beach Café that recently opened on the other end of Ocean Beach at 45th and Sloat, across from the Zoo. Only this time, he got paid in cash, not sandwiches.

In addition to surfers, you'll also find bike riders, people from other neighborhoods, and families—many of them regulars. On the celebrity end of the scale, actor Benjamin Bratt (who surfs and lives in San Francisco) used to come in almost everyday. There have been some Tracy Chapman sightings, and Dennis Quaid visited, as did Carel Struycken, the-seven-foot-tall Dutch actor you may remember from his portrayal of Lurch in *The Addams Family*, as well as his appearance in *Men in Black*, *Witches of Eastwick*, and the *Star Trek* and *Twin Peaks* TV shows. William B. Davis, the infamous Cigarette Smoking Man from *The X-Files* has also dropped by Java Beach.

Because Java Beach has become a community center, city politicians show up from time to time—such as former Hizzoner, the youthful Gavin Newsom. This is still a chuckle for many who knew the neighborhood's reputation before Java Beach opened.

One of the former Animals also paid a visit. "He had done a 15-year prison sentence, got out, and come back here," explained Pat. He said to me, 'Hey, bro, where's everybody at?'

"'They're gone.'

"'Gone? Where'd they go?'

"'They're dead.' And I wasn't kidding, except for one or two who got sober and a couple in prison.

"He says, 'Bro, you got a beer?' I gave him a beer. He knocked it back in one long sip. Then says, 'I'm out of here, bro.' That was the last I saw of him.

"It was the Twilight Zone for him," continued Pat. "The Animals were gone; the tunnel filled in. But I'm still here and I own this place, which made it even weirder because I was one of the guys in that tunnel drinking beer. I was a real party animal. I always had a 12-pack with me—a street fighter—one of the Sunset Boys. (He grew up at 44th and Kirkham.) The thing is, I came from a good family and went to good schools. But I could run in any crowd.

"My dad passing away when we were young was one of the reasons for the drinking and the hanging out. Suffering losses and grief when you're young kind of puts you in a desert," explained Pat. Pat speaks with the laser-like focus and clarity of a guy who's been through some stuff. He says he could have gone either way—lucky for him, and the community, he chose the right direction.

Pat also spearheaded the effort to create a small park out of the vacant lot filled with broken glass and dog poop across the street from the café. This is the very lot he looked across, years ago, when he had his vision of Java Beach.

Now that you're familiar with Java Beach Café and the neighborhood, you might want to explore Ocean Beach itself. It has numerous personalities—cold and windy when the famous San Francisco fog is in and inviting on those less frequent warm and sunny days when it thinks it's a Southern California beach. Either way, it's never crowded and three miles long (running from Balboa Street to Sloat Boulevard, paralleling the Great Highway). If you're looking for splendid solitude, this is the place. For swimming, however, it's not the place—there are lots of tides and currents. Leave getting wet to the intrepid surfers.

On your Ocean Beach walk, you might have a shipwreck sighting—that is, what's left of the three-masted clipper ship called *King George*. Constructed in Maine during the mid-1850s, it spent much of its inglorious life hauling manure fertilizer across the oceans of the world. As the story goes, a tug pulled the *King George* through the Golden Gate on January 25, 1878, and then left it at anchor to help a distressed ship. In the meantime, the anchor drifted, and the clipper ran aground on Ocean Beach where Noriega Street ends. Its remains have been there ever since.

From time to time, when the conditions are right to wash away the sand, the V-shaped bow and stern magically appear at the shoreline.

If you make it to the end of the beach, visit the new Java Beach Café at 2650 Sloat Boulevard (corner of 45th Avenue). Look for the following landmark on the median strip across from the café: an oddball, fully restored, seven-foot-high, 350-pound, fiberglass Doggie Diner head (a smiling dachshund wearing a chef's hat and bow tie). You may or may not know about Doggie Diner, the popular Bay Area chain of fast-food eateries, started in 1948 by Al Ross. He opened his first diner near an Oakland high school, serving hot dogs, grilled cheese, hamburgers, pastrami sandwiches, and the like. By the 1960s, Ross had 26 Doggie Diners, including 13 in San Francisco (one at 2750 Sloat Boulevard, just down from Java Beach). His slogans were "We compete in quality not price" and "There is nothing finer than the Doggie Diner."

A guy named Harold Bachman designed the famous doggie head icons for Ross in 1965, and, at one time, some of them actually rotated. Unfortunately, about thirty years after he began, Ross sold the successful chain to a corporate entity, which ran it into the ground and closed the diners in 1986.

Across from Java Beach Café, at the corner of Sloat Boulevard and the Great Highway, sits the San Francisco Zoo. Its parking lot was, back in the day, the location of an aquatic wonder of the world—the Fleishhacker Pool.

Imagine a swimming pool measuring 160-feet wide by 1,000-feet long, 14-feet deep underneath the diving platform, holding six-and-a-half million gallons of water, with 12 lifeguards on duty, including some patrolling in rowboats, and a capacity for 10,000 swimmers. This is what entrepreneur and philanthropist Herbert Fleishhacker built next to Ocean Beach at a cost of $1,500,000.

It laid claim to the title of largest heated saltwater pool in the world (the water being warmed to 72°F and filtered). On opening day, April 22, 1925, Fleishhacker Pool hosted a swim meet featuring Johnny Weissmuller, world champion Olympic freestyler. It was watched by a crowd of 5,000 people. Weissmuller made other appearances at the Fleishhhaker Pool after he became famous for his twelve Tarzan films—the first one being the 1932 vehicle *Tarzan, the Ape Man*. (He's still the best Tarzan.) Post Tarzan, from the late 1940s to the mid 1950s, Weissmuller starred in the Jungle Jim movies and TV series.

Esther Williams—the champion swimmer, 1940 Olympic team member, and actress— is another celebrity that occasionally visited the pool. She and Weissmuller worked together in the 1940 San Francisco Aquacade review at the Golden Gate Exposition when producer Billy Rose tapped the unknown Williams to appear opposite the popular screen star. It's said that Tarzan himself chose her from a casting call of 75 swimmers.

Alas, the large pool's popularity fell off over the years, due mainly to the cool unbeach-like weather at Ocean Beach. In 1981, it was broken up and filled with debris—and sadly, became a zoo parking lot (and a memory) in 2002.

After all this walking on the beach and waltzing down memory lane, you've probably worked up an appetite worthy of the hearty fare at either Java Beach. Fill your tank in the AM with oatmeal, raisins, and golden flax seed; a big bad (and fresh) hummus veggie bagel; or a very large bowl of granola with Greek yogurt and fresh fruit. The microroasted coffees (either espresso or American style) go nicely with all of the above.

Java Beach has overhauled its coffee—moving quickly, as Pat Maguire described it—into the third wave of espresso brewing. The first wave being Folgers in a percolator; the second—Starbucks and dark-roasted Peets; and the third, the new batch of up-and-coming microroasters. Pat hand selects his beans and has them medium-roasted in small batches by a master coffee roaster in Marin County. The result is a smooth drop that won't give you acid stomach.

Pat also pays special attention to his baristas—often a large bump on the road to a good espresso. He hires only experienced people, who know how to draw a proper shot (short with nice crema) and steam the milk so that the foam is silky.

For lunch, try one of the world-famous (well, at least Ocean Beach-famous) really good hot sub sandwiches: the Tsunami (ham, mortadella, salami, and melted cheese on a Dutch crunch roll with mayo, mustard, lettuce, tomato, red onion, special sauce); BBQ Chicken (chicken breast smothered in barbeque sauce and melted cheese), and Whirling Dervish Veggie (melted feta, tomato, mixed greens, drizzled with balsamic vinegar and oil).

Or maybe you're after a brewski. There's Guinness, Sierra Nevada, Fat Tire, Hefeweizen, or Budweiser on tap and happy hour from 5 to 7PM. Grab a pitcher and watch the sunset.

Life is good at Java Beach.

You need a trip to Ocean Beach at the edge of North America, where all that's between you and Hawaii is a lot of Pacific Ocean. Hop on the N Judah streetcar (be careful; they run in packs) and ride it through the Sunset District to the end of the line. Then look for Java Beach written in neon on a very cool surfboard sign. You're at Java Beach Café, where you'll enjoy pastries and smooth microroasted coffee (cappuccino with creamy foam and a short, Italian-style shot of espresso) alongside a variety of folks: surfers, locals, and a smattering of tourists. The specialty of the house is the hot sub sandwich (Tsunami, BBQ Chicken, Bonfire Delight, Whirling Dervish). It's both big and good, so it can fuel surfers and beach walkers with ease. There's also an array of deli sandwiches, salads, hot soups, along with wine and beer. This is a real neighborhood place—owned by Pat Maguire, his wife, Buffy, and their three little boys, Kevin, Connor, and Dylan.

Arizmendi Bakery

1331 9th Avenue
(415) 566-3117
7AM–7PM, Tuesday to Friday
7:30AM–6PM, Saturday
7:30AM–5PM, Sunday
Closed Monday
www.arizmendibakery.org

What is the Cheese Board? (A) A board for slicing cheese. (B) A small group of people who are in charge of the world's cheese. (C) A cheese shop that opened in 1967 and expanded into a worker-owned-and-operated neighborhood cheese shop, bakery, and pizzeria in Berkeley, California.

If you guessed (C), you're correct. And you also just identified the mother ship of Arizmendi Bakery in San Francisco. The Cheese Board has helped launch a group of independent worker cooperatives, based on its business model, by offering training, seed money, and recipes. (There are also Arizmendi bakeries in Oakland, Emeryville, and San Rafael.)

The name comes from Jose Maria Arizmendiarrieta (Arizmendi for short), a young Spanish priest who believed passionately in social justice and worker-owned-and-operated businesses. In 1941, he was sent as an educator to Mondragon, a Basque town economically savaged by the Spanish Civil War. It had a population of 8,000 and one small factory.

Fifteen years later, inspired by his vision, five engineering graduates (and former students of the padre) bought a small stove factory with money borrowed from the community. This 25-employee business spawned today's Mondragon Cooperatives—100 worker-owned enterprises and affiliated organizations employing 34,000 employees.

Indirectly, you can thank Padre Arizmendi for the rustic artisan goodies you sample at this bakery. The sign over the kitchen reads: "Make Loaves Not War"—in this vein, the tasty bread is a good place to start. It's hearty (but not too heavy) and excellent. Choose from a long list, including Irish soda, multigrain, provolone olive, garlic sourdough, corn cheddar, and fig fennel sourdough.

You'll also want to sample one of the thin sourdough crust pizzas, which have a great following (regulars buy them one slice at a time). Every day there's a different flavor, such as arugula, roasted red bell peppers, Manchego cheese, garlic oil, parsley, and Parmesan; mixed fresh bell peppers, goat cheese, garlic oil, fresh cilantro; or house-made tomato sauce, green olives, feta cheese, rosemary oil, and Italian parsley.

Moving from savory to sweet, Arizmendi makes a very tasty granola, using, among other things, the nuts and brown sugar residue left over in the sticky buns baking pan. And the shortbread cookies (plain or ginger) would impress even your Scottish grandmother. They deliver a rich buttery flavor, building on four simple ingredients: fresh butter, sugar, a smidge of salt, and a little flour.

In the muffin department, there's pumpkin praline, banana walnut, apple walnut, and lemon poppy seed—rivaled by the Arizmendi scones, especially the grainy and eccentric corn/cherry (this combo: who would have thought) and the masterpiece oat scone. It tastes

so good that the ingredients must include something naughty. And they do. As Arizmendi member Diane Glaub, a fun lady in a baseball cap, combined ingredients in a gigantic mixer, she explained, "I'm combining oats, whole wheat flour, a little white flour, brown sugar, baking soda powder, currants, unsalted butter (big chunks), buttermilk, and heavy whipping cream. We make a big batch of dry mix from scratch, for the week, then portion it out, and the last step is adding the butter, whipping cream, and buttermilk. We make about 80 oat scones per day." (They bake a total of 460 to 500 scones daily, including all varieties.)

Diane is one of the original worker/owners—a friend told her about the place at the time it was opening in a former fast photo shop. "So I came by, and there were two gals sitting outside with a table, some baguettes, and some information," said Diane who worked

as a gardener and also had previous experience with scratch baking (as in everything from scratch, no mixes). "They were trying to attract people who would be interested in owning and operating a cooperative bakery."

You also need to know that this is more than just a bread and breakfast pastry institution, especially from the week before Thanksgiving through the week between Christmas and New Year's Eve, when Arizmendi produces an array of special treats, including pecan pies, pumpkin tea cake, and its famous Yule log (with faux bark frosting).

Heather Ferne, who started in 2004, pushed the group to expand in the cake direction, and was especially influential in developing the popular (I-really-shouldn't-eat-the-entire-piece) chocolate fudge cake, with either chocolate or salted caramel frosting, which, luckily for you, is available all year round. She said, "I love making cakes… that's my thing. Wedding cakes, birthday cakes, all kinds. Cakes are refined, and I like the finishing aspect of making a cake look stunning and then having it taste just as good as it looks." Heather attended the San Francisco California Culinary Academy from 1993 to 1994, followed by work in a Michigan hotel, a small family-owned bakery, the Safeway bakery, a restaurant, and a family-run catering company. As she said, "I kind of just did it all."

Let's say you want to work at Arizmendi—the important thing to digest is that no one is the boss. How could that be, you ask? Well, there's no hierarchy, and the wage is the same for people who started on day one and those hired last year. A profit-sharing benefit kicks in after six months, which is at the end of your probationary period, when you're voted in as a full member and owner of the bakery. You then accrue patronage (profit sharing) paid quarterly on top of the hourly rate. There's also a four-day work week, six week's vacation, a 401(k) plan, and a family health plan.

"I love that the children of the bakery members come in to see their moms and dads, and hang out and see what's going on in the bakery," said Heather. "This enriches the business and makes it more like a family business. These kids are going to grow up right here behind the scenes with all the flour." Sue Lopez, an original worker-owner and refugee from the arts, said: "We're turning into a nursery of sorts, with lots of baby boys… really large baby boys."

Heather adds, "We'll have a new dad in the bakery very soon—rumor is: it's a girl!"

Competition for each opening at Arizmendi is intense—around 80 applications, narrowed to 20 to 22 actual interviews, followed by tryouts in the kitchen. (A background in baking is not a prerequisite. Original worker/owner Kim McGee previously worked for an adult toy company.) Once you've got the job, you learn how to do everything so that everyone has the same skills, and you rotate through the committees that run the back of the house: financial, purchasing, production, and hiring and evaluations.

In the team-centered world of business, think of this as the ultimate team approach (20 members, aged 22 to 46). "You see the strengths of each person, and each of these contribute to the whole. With the right people, it works. We try to make decisions on the basis of consensus voting, and convince everyone to go in the same direction. If that doesn't happen, sometimes we just have to let it go. And let it be undecided," Heather said.

You, on the other hand, can be very decisive about where to head with your Arizmendi oat scone and cappuccino in hand. This Inner Sunset neighborhood (9th and Irving streets), with shops, restaurants, and cafés, sits on the edge of Golden Gate Park, and the San Francisco Botanical

Gardens at Strybing Arboretum, home to thousands of plants—California natives (both flora and fauna) and exotic species. After visiting the arboretum, saunter over to the nearby and charming Japanese Gardens, originally constructed as a Japanese Village for the 200-acre, 1894 California Midwinter International Exposition (shortened to the Midwinter Fair by the locals). The only other major remnant of the fair, inspired by the wildly successful 1893 Columbian Exposition in Chicago, is an open-air space, originally called the Court of Honor, and later renamed the Music Concourse. The Temple of Music (bandshell) at the far end of the concourse was dedicated in 1900. (A scene from Woody Allen's 1973 film *Play It Again Sam* was shot among the benches located in front of the stage.)

Right next door stands the very bold and controversial de Young Museum. Its tower rises up from the trees like a Mayan temple in Tikal—people either love it or hate it. You can spend days viewing the art collections and just soaking up the stunning interior. (The café is good, too.)

Across the street, more or less, you'll find the newly rebuilt and stunning California Academy of Sciences, designed by Renzo Piano and including a natural history museum, planetarium, and aquarium. And, not too far from there, walking east on John F. Kennedy Drive, you come across the Conservatory of Flowers, a large Victorian greenhouse, first opened in 1879 on the eastern edge of the new park. It has almost 17,000 windowpanes, in case you're counting.

If you need more exercise, take a very long walk out to Ocean Beach through the park, which measures three miles in length and a half-mile in width.

In 1870, when the idea to create Golden Gate Park got the green light, the entire area was a desolate section of the San Francisco peninsula—a barren, windswept, fogbound collection of sand dunes referred to as the Outside Lands. Not the greatest spot for a verdant rectangle of exotic vegetation, thought Frederick Olmsted Law, who had designed New York's Central Park and was asked to do something similar for San Francisco. He suggested instead a green belt of native vegetation that ran from the current Aquatic Park location on San Francisco Bay along the path of Van Ness Avenue and then turned west out to the ocean.

San Francisco had gone from 1,000 people just before the Gold Rush to 150,000 folks in 1879. The impetus for a civic playground came from both San Francisco's citizens and its wealthy land developers. This latter group saw that the main direction for the city's growth was west along the borders of the proposed park, which would increase property values. For them, Golden Gate Park equaled dollar signs.

The park's board of commissioners hired civil engineer William Hammond Hall to make a topographical survey in 1870; a year later, he became park superintendent. The park that he surveyed, however, was not Olmsted's vision—the city fathers and Hall preferred the Central Park model.

Land acquisition proved tricky because squatters claimed possession of certain areas of the proposed park. When everything was finally in place, construction of the park began in the fall of 1870, on its eastern end, at the Panhandle. Hall did retain one of Olmsted's tenets—to use as much of the natural topography as possible—a push back to those who wanted to flatten the entire landscape.

By the mid 1870s the park offered San Francisco's citizenry a combination of bridle paths, promenades, and drives for their outdoor enjoyment. Ten years later, three streetcar lines reached the park, and it is estimated that 45,000 people visited the park during one day in April of 1886. The residential areas on either side of the park's eastern end sprang up and immediately became desirable locations.

As the park was developed, certain of its aspects sparked controversy, one of these being the casino/restaurant that opened in 1881 near the Conservatory of Flowers. It attracted a rowdy element and was later moved away from the conservatory and enlarged with a second story, in an effort to attract a better mannered clientele. It went bust a year later, in 1891, ending up for a while as a stuffed animal museum.

Another controversial matter: the park was gated at sunset, which made lots of San Franciscans unhappy. There was much back and forth about the reasons for this. One point of view, as presented in an 1881 newspaper editorial, suggested that an open park encouraged hugging in the dark among young couples, leading to more intense (and scandalous) physical contact, not to mention "late-night huggers" are not alert and productive at work the next morning. The other side simply thought the gate was stupid. Eventually, it was removed.

The park's popularity continued to increase, along with ease of access. By the early 1900s, nine streetcar lines ended there, and automobiles were allowed in the park.

Crusty Scotsman John McLaren (born in 1846) became park superintendent in 1890, a post he kept until well past the mandatory retirement age of 70, when he was appointed superintendent for life. He died in 1943. Gothic-style McLaren Lodge, his home and office, built in 1896 (the Addams Family could happily settle in here), sits at the entrance of the park, and is now the headquarters for the San Francisco Recreation and Parks Department. Like William Hammond Hall, McLaren believed in working with the forces of nature, as much as possible, and followed the course set for the park by his predecessor.

Just like the park, Arizmendi is bustling on weekends. Most of the customers are regulars, and many live in the area. One of the more well known is actor (and San Francisco native) Benjamin Bratt. There is also the occasional high-profile out-of-towner looking for a good scone—such as Rosalind Carter, who came in one day accompanied by guys in dark suits talking into their sleeves.

This little bakery has come a long way since it first opened on Friday, October 13, 2000, a date not known for good luck. "Prior to opening, as part of training, we were doing these things called dry runs—basically baking product and giving it away. So once we opened for business, people didn't understand, and said, 'Oh they aren't giving it away any more,'" explained Diane Glaub.

Arizmendi bakeries flourish by sticking to their original business plan, described by Sue Lopez: "Bank roll the next business, train the workers, take people in as interns, do your own thing, and share the wealth, which is not really the capitalist model."

So you've decided to "hang" in Golden Gate Park—whoa, you've got your hands full. There is much to see and do (Japanese Tea Garden, Arboretum, Academy of Science, de Young Museum, and a herd of buffalo in the Buffalo Paddock). You better stock up on supplies. The Arizmendi Bakery, a worker-owned cooperative, lives in the cool, casual, Inner Sunset neighborhood at 9th and Irving, just below UC Med Center. Grab a couple of slices of pizza to take with you, a few oat scones, and a chunk of chocolate fudge cake for later. (Use your BlackBerry, iPhone, or whatever phone to see a detailed bread and pizza schedule on their website: arizmendibakery.org). Try the chai from a spiced orange-peel-and-pepper recipe developed by one of the worker/owners. Freshly baked, all natural ingredients, reasonably priced. Life is good. Life is simple. Well, not really, but you'll find a small oasis here.

Mojo Bicycle Café

639-A Divisadero Street
www.mojobicyclecafe.com

Café
(415) 440-2370
7AM–10PM, **Monday to Wednesday**
7AM–midnight, **Thursday & Friday**
8AM–midnight, **Saturday**
8AM–5PM, **Sunday**

Bike Shop
(415) 440-2338
10AM–6PM, **Monday, Tuesday,**
    Friday, Saturday
11AM–6PM, **Wednesday**
Noon–6PM, Sunday
Closed Thursday

*H*ybrid cars are good, so why not a hybrid café—one that helps you pedal and not pollute, and refuel yourself in the bargain. Mojo Bicycle Café. What's the name "Mojo" all about? Here is the mission statement straight from the Mojo website:

Bicycles mean many different things to many different people—and that's how we like it. Whatever your reasons for wanting to get on a bike, we've got love for you. At a time when

fossil fuel addiction makes driving a gas-powered vehicle seem like planetary suicide, the
bicycle makes undeniable sense. It's one way to arrest the downward spiral.

We have much more in common as cyclists than whatever differences we may have as people.
Bicycling is about good mojo—and Mojo is about good bikes.

Mojo Bicycle Café is the offspring of three dudes: Remy Nelson, John McDonnell, and
Dave Robb. They met while working in a San Francisco bike shop, and hired each other (sort
of). Dave hired John as a service manager and, later, John hired Remy (then a high school
senior) as an intern. He was the new guy, the kid—sometimes they'd send him to buy beer
from the Armenian guy at the corner store, who'd always ask, "This is for John and Dave, right?"

It was over a beer that the three hatched the idea for Mojo. Originally seen as a beer
garden/bike shop in their mind's eye, it morphed into a bike shop café with beer, wine,

coffee, and food. They eventually went their
separate ways; however, says Remy, "I think I was
the one who persevered and finally said, 'Let's
do this.'" In the meantime, he finished college,
worked, saved money, and traveled around the
world—still thinking about the bike shop.

Seven years passed and he contacted John
and Dave, with a solid plan to take things past
the "good idea" stage. Remy and his parents had
bought a run-down Victorian on Divisadero
Street. Upstairs was a four-bedroom apartment,
which he renovated, and downstairs, an art
gallery space—the designated future home
of Mojo, but also in need of much work. "We
took out everything but the hardwood floor—

replaced the plumbing and electrical," explained John. "We painted. We had the foundation repaired and took the old brick from the foundation, and turned the chicken-bone-and-broken-glass-filled backyard into a garden. We did way too much ourselves."

By the time the renovations were completed, the building had been redone inside and out—including burning a quarter inch of lead paint from the exterior. Mojo's first home, a 1906 earthquake survivor built in 1890, never looked so good.

At some point during the reconstruction, Mojo took on its hybrid self as two different entities: John began to take care of the bike shop, and Remy focused on the café. While the boys knew bikes (and beer), they didn't really know food. "The food was a process," explained Remy. "Originally, we only wanted to have beer. But it turns out that if you want to sell alcohol and allow people under 21 to walk in the front door, you have to serve food. So I had to make up a menu for the ABC (Alcoholic Beverage Commission), and then show them that we could actually make this stuff."

Lucky for you, the light menu that Remy invented includes some pretty good stuff. Here's a sampling for breakfast—bagels with anything from cream cheese to hummus to pesto or lox and tomatoes; hearty breakfast bagels à la egg or egg and sausage; that old standby, oatmeal with brown sugar, cinnamon, raisins, and almonds; and summery yogurt, granola, and fresh fruit.

Lunch and dinner features the spicy Le Marocain, a baguette of harissa (red pepper paste), aioli, turkey, melted gruyère, roasted bell peppers, cucumber, and lettuce. The fresh mozzarella-and-heirloom-tomato-stuffed Caprese comes with basil, pesto, balsamic vinegar, and olive oil. During the winter, roasted red pepper fills in for the tomato. For the open-face sandwich crowd, Mojo offers Le Croque-Mojo—French ham, gruyère, roasted bell pepper, cucumber, and lettuce on toasted bread.

Your beverage essentials—espresso, cappuccino, and macchiato—are made with coffee from De La Paz and Ritual Coffee Roasters. Standouts in the beer department: Reality Czech Pilsner, a delicate soft lager from Moonlight Brewing Company located in nearby Santa Rosa, and Big Daddy IPA by Speakeasy Ales & Lagers, a robust India pale ale from San Francisco

that will challenge your taste buds to a duel. Mojo is one of the top ten sellers of Big Daddy IPA. The brewery now exports pallets of Big Daddy to the East Coast and overseas.

"A lot of people come in the café, and they have no idea there's actually a bike shop back there," said Remy. But that won't happen to you, and a good thing, too. Because these guys are bike dorks with a great selection of bikes, and without the attitude—they won't talk down to you.

Mojo sells bikes that fall into three general categories. John describes them: "Comfort bikes give you flat handle bars higher than the saddle, upright riding position, road-size wheels but a little fatter tires, lots of gears, and stronger brakes. The road bike has an aggressive racy riding position, defined by drop handlebars, and tall narrow wheels. And for off-road, the mountain bike… with knobby tires and beefed-up suspension."

If you want brand names, there's Jamis, Kona, and Swobo. The focus of this neighborhood shop is city riders, and fun, practical, cool bikes; however, you will find some high-end machines here. And speaking of expensive bikes, you may not know that most Italian racers are now made in China. "Chinese bikes are really good—even the high-end, carbon fiber, 16-pound racing bikes are good," explained John. "Chinese have always been able to make a good cheap bike, but only in the past five years have they emerged as a top-end manufacturer. You can't beat the pricing."

For coolness (and daredevilosity), check out the fixed-gear bike. It's a road bike with one gear, no brakes, and a rear wheel that drives the pedals. Thus, you can't stop pedaling, and to slow or stop, you have to stand on the pedals and skid. At the turn of the 19th century, fixed-gear bike racers were the equivalent of the overpaid millionaire athletes of today. Some earned in the low six figures each year for their high-speed antics at the velodrome, an arena with a banked track for racing fixed-gear bicycles.

In 1879, a former railroad shed was transformed into Madison Square Garden, and used as a velodrome. By 1890, a larger and better Madison Square Garden featured big-time fixed-gear bike races as part of a national racing circuit.

A hundred plus years later, bike messengers, who tend to be edge-pushing rebels and adrenaline junkies, made the fixed-gear popular again. John explained, "A couple bike messengers in New York started using them 25 years ago because the city is dead flat. From there, it has spread. Nothing can really explain the phenomenon… It's a fashion statement now. Kids will buy these bikes and get the rims colored to match hubs, frames, belts, and hats."

Dave Robb, who John describes as the third head of the three-headed monster, used a fixed-gear bike when he was a bike messenger in Boston. "I'd go to the postal annex and pick up four or five mail bins, nested on my handlebars, in the snow, on my fixed gear. A good thing about a fixed gear is that you can ride very slow and still keep your balance. You're constantly pedaling and putting weight into the bike. You don't have any dead spots like on a bike with a freewheel. The bike is always balancing," explained Dave.

Dave has three daughters and describes himself as the procreator of the bunch. Before getting into the bike biz, he was, believe it or not, the guy who would open Starbucks's new stores. It happened this way: in the late 1980s and 1990s, Dave worked for a company called Coffee Connections (kind of like Peets, only in Boston), which was bought by Starbucks. He started traveling around the country opening stores, eventually burned out on the corporate scene, moved back to Boston, and became a bike messenger.

"John and I lived parallel lives in different locations," Dave said. He was in Boston at roughly the same time John worked as a bike messenger in Washington, DC. Their paths finally crossed at a San Francisco bike shop in 1997.

Back in the day, John had his share of bike messenger adventures. Once he tangled with a guy in a courier truck, who ran him off the road and came at him with a crowbar. He later learned that this guy had moved from Philly to DC, trying to get out of the mob. Ironically, they both worked for the same company.

Another time, the U.S. Capitol Police chased him. "They were trying to pull me over, on foot, for a traffic ticket, and I was really busy, so I took off on the first cop who lunged at me. He missed and fell flat on his face. I started shooting down Capitol Hill," said John. "He was really mad, and he radioed to his buddy who jumped out from behind a truck to grab me, but he didn't do the math about my speed. I was going 30 miles an hour. I put my hand up, plowed into him, and then hopped back on my bike. They were chasing me in cruisers, too, but I finally got away. I later had to shave my head and change bikes for a while."

Juggling file boxes is a required skill for bike messengers. John occasionally got a delivery from a lobbyist with one envelope for every member of congress. He'd balance the boxes on his handlebars and back rack, maxed out at 150 pounds.

Sometimes the small deliveries involved big bucks. "I had a regular once-a-week run, a shoebox size thing," explained John. "I'd shake it and it seemed empty. I got very curious about what was in the box. It finally got the better of me, and I opened it—there was a check for 1.6 million." Then there's the really big bucks delivery—Dave once ran a multi-million dollar bearer bond from a law firm to a bank.

And sometimes, the smaller deliveries were the strangest—Dave said that a friend used to messenger anonymous body parts, such as eyeballs.

Once you've supped in the café and checked out the bikes, you might want to eyeball nearby Alamo Square, a pleasant little park, one block up from Divisadero Street toward downtown San Francisco. It was one of the parks used as a refugee camp after the 1906 earthquake and fire, along with Washington Square and Mission Dolores Park. You probably recognize Alamo Square for the "Painted Ladies" that border it on the Steiner Street side. These are not women of easy virtue from the Old West, but instead a row of charming Victorian homes that escaped the great post-earthquake conflagration (halted at Van Ness Avenue) and have, over the years, been photographed, ad naseum, in postcards and TV spots. They have also shown up in the opening sequence for the sitcom *Full House* (1987–1995) starring Bob Saget, and as one of the locations in *Invasion of the Body Snatchers* (1978).

Originally built by carpenter/builder Matthew Kavanaugh between 1892 and 1896, the seven famous Victorians sold for around $3,500 each, which today probably wouldn't cover the cost of repainting. (Kavanaugh liked the neighborhood—his own mansion, part of the row, is open to the public.) The houses were painted with three or more bright contrasting colors initially, and then, in the early part of the 1900s, for some reason the color scheme switched to grey, black, and white. However, since the 1970s, color is back, and you can see these ladies in their glory.

Mostly neighborhood folks hang out here. Maybe they have a bike, maybe they don't, and maybe they eventually buy one from Mojo. It's all good as far as Remy, John, and Dave are concerned. These are cool guys, and good friends. How cool? Gary Fisher, mountain bike champion and the guy who built the first mountain bike, comes in, and so does female bike designer Sky Yaeger. The eats here include tasty baguettes and sandwiches, fresh organic greens and produce, and brand names Brown Cow yogurt and Kettle Chips. Beverages feature Big Daddy IPA, Reality Czech Pilsner, and pretty good coffee. Just up the hill, see the Painted Lady Victorians lining famous Alamo Square. The neighborhood, on the edge of the Western Addition, used to be marginal, but it's transitioning toward the better. There's even one of the city's new parklets right in front.

· 4 ·

MISSION DISTRICT

*L*otta' life here—where blue-collar Mission Street and hipster Valencia Street rub elbows. This area is often warm and sunny when the rest of San Francisco is fog city. Some of the Mission still feels a bit shady (i.e., the 16th Street BART stop), but you'll know when you're somewhere you shouldn't be. As you wander from popular Dolores Park (a refugee encampment of temporary cottages after the 1906 earthquake) down to 24th Street and the colorful murals of Balmy Alley, you'll find coffee, gelato, good eats—and a vibrant Latino community. Hard to believe that 250 years ago there was a medium-sized freshwater lake in the heart of the Mission.

Bi-Rite Creamery & Bakeshop

3692 18th Street (at Dolores)
(415) 626-5600
11AM–10PM, Sunday to Thursday
11AM–11PM, Friday & Saturday
www.biritecreamery.com

*I*f you like really good American-style ice cream, then you need to get in here. The Bi-Rite ladies—owners Anne Walker and Kris Hoogerhyde—handcraft all their products in small batches using mostly local organic ingredients, and then serve them in biodegradable packaging. (They have a conscience about these things.)

Anne and Kris met in a restaurant kitchen, where both were pastry chefs. At one point (pre Bi-Rite Creamery), they were baking for Bi-Rite Market, located across the street from the creamery. This involved renting a kitchen, baking everything there, and then driving the goods a mile and a half to the market.

By the way, Bi-Rite Market is someplace not to miss, either. It opened in 1940, as a corner store, and since 1964, has been owned by Anne's in-laws, the Mogannam family. Her husband, Sam, and his brother, Raphael, took over Bi-Rite in 1997 and restored its classic look, including the art deco façade and original neon sign. Inside, you'll find a full-service grocery store that offers a range of products from artisan specialties such as hand-harvested wild rice to your everyday bunch of bananas.

During the search for another baking space closer to Bi-Rite Market, Anne and Kris came across their present location. They decided, however, that they did not want to open just another bakery. "What was missing in the neighborhood was an ice cream shop. So we're actually a bakery and an ice cream shop," explained Anne.

"Not many places in the City make their own ice cream," added Kris. "Anne and I made ice cream in restaurants, and when we discussed opening this place, we were, of course, going to make our own base. Then we realized that we go through almost 100 gallons of base a week. So labor-wise, we'd be spending most of our time making ice cream base and pasteurizing it. We found a base that was just as good as any that we could make."

The base is the foundation for ice cream: milk, cream, egg yolks, and sugar. Luckily, the Bi-Rite ladies discovered that Marin County's Straus diary makes a fantastic ice cream base from all organic ingredients and delivers it in ready-to-go gallon containers—saving them a lot of work.

In 1941, German-born Bill Straus began farming with 23 cows on the shores of Tomales Bay, about 60 miles north of San Francisco. Over the years, his wife, Ellen Straus, a World War II refugee from the Netherlands, became the force behind the family's strong commitment to farmland protection and other environmental issues. She was the co-founder of Marin Agricultural Land Trust (MALT), an agricultural conservation easement program that has helped save many West Marin family farms and ranches from development (more than 40,000 acres to be exact) since its inception in 1980.

Oldest son Albert took the Straus farm in a new direction by converting it to a certified organic dairy in 1993, and renaming it the Straus Family Creamery, producing organic milk, yogurt, butter, and ice cream. A year later it became the first certified organic dairy west of the Mississippi River. (It takes one year to fully certify a dairy herd to produce organic milk.) Locals rave about the products, as do not-so locals, such as Martha Stewart, who featured Straus products on her TV show and said they were "extraordinary."

Anne and Kris create all the flavor components from scratch, using as many local, organic, and sustainable products as possible. The coffee for coffee toffee ice cream comes from Ritual Coffee Roasters (also in this book) located, more or less, down the street. And, they make their own marshmallows and chocolate-covered almonds for Rocky Road.

"The really fun part is seeing what's in the area and what we can use. We have a honey lavender ice cream with honey from Mint Hill," said Anne. Floral-tasting Mint Hill honey comes from beehives located in the Castro District of San Francisco, and takes its name from the nearby United States Mint (built in 1937) at 155 Hermann Street.

Flavors change with the seasons. In the spring and summer, Anne and Kris get organic strawberries from a farm just north of Santa Cruz, and their balsamic strawberry ice cream becomes all the rage with customers. Last winter, they concocted a holiday special: brown sugar ice cream with a ginger caramel swirl.

While orange cardamom is Kris's personal favorite, many customers prefer the salted caramel. "From day one it was the most popular," said Kris. "It's the perfect balance of bitter, sweet, and salty." They go through 150 pints a week, all hand packed.

Here's how you make salted caramel. (Don't try this without adult supervision.) Put the sugar directly into a pan. Heat it slowly so it dissolves. It should have a frothy top, start to boil around the edges, and become a dark smoky color. Add some cream, and then salt. After it cools down, stir it into your base, and put it in your batch freezer.

Bi-Rite uses an Emery Thompson batch freezer, which is a large freezing chamber that mixes, agitates, and freezes the ice cream mixture. A man named Emery Thompson invented and patented the first mechanized vertical batch freezer in 1905, and, believe it or not, Emery Thompson machines are still one-hundred-percent made in America.

"When we first opened, we made all of the ice cream. And then we just got so busy—we couldn't make the ice cream, do the bakery, and run the business," explained Kris. "So we now have a full-time ice cream maker," adds Anne, "Kris and I create all of the flavors for everything we serve." (The two Bi-Rite ladies often finish each other's sentences.) In addition to a full-time ice cream maker, they employ five bakers and a number of scoopers.

When Bi-Rite opened in early 2007, Anne was seven months pregnant, which she said, "Was a little crazy."

"We had long days in the beginning, and now when I work an eight-hour day, I think I'm leaving early," added Kris.

Both claim that their great staff makes things a lot easier now. Either Anne or Kris opens in the morning, and a staff member closes at night. Their philosophy: if you're going to run a successful small business, you need lots of support. Otherwise, you're going to run yourself into the ground.

What do the Bi-Rite ladies do outside of work? Anne said, "I have two small children, so that's what I do."

"Actually, I think of the ice cream shop as my small child. Or all the employees as my children," added Kris. "With both of us, food is a big part of our life."

"Both of our husbands are in the food world. That's one of the reasons we live in San Francisco," continued Anne.

Kris summed it up nicely: "Nothing like a good cocktail and a good meal, that's what I say." She also likes camping and hiking.

When you're standing in line for your cone or sundae, you might rub elbows with someone famous. Actors Owen Wilson and Kate Hudson came in, as did singer Tracy Chapman. And Kris admits to flirting shamelessly with Sam Rockwell one night. "He's easy on the eyes. I didn't recognize him at first. He was very friendly. And short," she explained. "After he left, I turned to one of the scoopers and said, 'That's Sam Rockwell. You know, *Confessions of a Dangerous Mind*.' And their reply was, 'I wondered why you leapt across the counter to give him a sample.'"

But mostly the customers are locals, tourists, and people who come to hang out in Dolores Park, the 13.7-acre (two-block long and one-block wide) neighborhood open space. You can see the park from Bi-Rite's front door.

In the early fall of 1906, you would have noticed rows of 15 feet by 25 feet, olive drab cottages filling Dolores Park. It became a refugee camp for 1,600 homeless families after the devastating 7.9-magnitude earthquake (and ensuing fire) that began on April 18, at 5:12AM. Rental of a cottage came to roughly two dollars per month, per room, which went toward its purchase (paid off in about a year).

The rub, however, was a typical bureaucratic Catch-22—as soon as an individual owned the cottage, it had to be moved because it was illegal to have a private structure in a public park. Thus, the late summer of 1907 became a scene of people moving their structures by horse-drawn wagons to new locations. This exodus took place all over the city. At one time, every park and public open public space was filled with tents and these temporary cottages. There were 225,000 homeless out of a population of 400,000.

Dolores Park takes its name from nearby Mission Dolores (16th and Dolores streets), founded in 1776 and the city's oldest building. The Jewish Congregation Sherith Israel purchased the land for a cemetery in 1861. It closed in 1894, and the city of San Francisco bought the land for Dolores Park (paying $300,000), just in time for the earthquake.

In the period between the establishment of Mission Dolores and the Gold Rush, the Mission District remained sparsely populated and fairly remote—the center of town was located two miles away, over steep sand hills. Eventually, residents discovered the relatively fog-free Mission, with summer sunshine and willowy flowing creeks. Two plank roads (dirt roads covered crossways with 8- to 16-feet-long planks) were built around 1850. One, called the Mission Road, started in the Happy Valley neighborhood at Mission and First streets, running southwest along present-day Mission Street. (In 1852, there was a five-story sand hill near Mission and 5th streets.)

The other plank road began in St. Ann's Valley near the corner of Powell and Market streets (the current cablecar turnaround) and wound its way past the future location of the Civic Center. These two roads connected at what remained of the Mission Dolores site. The area quickly developed into the city's playground, with amusements such as bear and bull fighting—usually involving a bear tethered to a long chain in the middle of an arena and a bull roaming free. There were also two racecourses, all situated, ironically, near the old mission church.

The Bi-Rite Creamery & Bakeshop ladies—Anne and Kris—try to make a small impact on the environment by using easily composted cups and spoons, and little metal spoons for tasting their ice cream. On the other hand, they're trying to make a big impact on you with baked goods such as buttermilk upside-down cake and bittersweet chocolate soufflé cake. And, of course, their popular ice cream—salted caramel, double ginger, honey, roasted banana (which involves organic bananas and caramelized brown sugar)… the list goes on and on. To sample everything, you might need to stop in here twice a day. The new, expanded Bi-Rite includes a soft serve window, featuring Straus Dairy soft serve ice cream, along with muffins, cinnamon sticks, and chocolate cupcakes.

Mission Beach Café

198 Guerrero Street (at 14th Street)
(415) 861-0198
7AM–10PM, Monday to Thursday
7AM–11PM, Friday
9AM–11PM, Saturday
9AM–6PM, Sunday
www.missionbeachcafesf.com

The Mission District is not renowned for its beach life—however, there was, at one time, a medium-sized freshwater lake not too far from this café. If you stood in the middle of Laguna de Manantial (also called Laguna de los Dolores) 250 years ago, located at what is now the corner of 17th and Mission streets, you would have been about 15 feet underwater. The lake extended roughly two blocks in all directions. Some historical documents suggest that it was filled in by the early 1800s.

On April 5, 1776, Captain Juan Bautista de Anza and his party of soldiers rowed up Mission Creek from San Francisco Bay to find a suitable spot for Mission Dolores near the lake's shore at 16th and Dolores streets. The creek remained navigable until 1874. After the 1906 earthquake, most of it was filled in with earthquake rubble and trash, and then eventually built on.

Mission Beach Café also sits on the former doorstep of Woodward's Gardens, a popular zoo/museum/amusement park that took up two city blocks (bordered by 13th, 15th, Valencia, and Mission streets) from 1866–1891. Owner Robert B. Woodward came west

from Rhode Island during the Gold Rush, and like most who struck it rich, he did so by serving the miners who themselves mostly ended up with empty pockets.

Woodward opened a hotel for men only called What Cheer House in 1852, located at Sacramento and Leidesdorff streets, which is now in the shadow of the Pyramid Building. In spite of the fact that it had a no-alcohol policy, it very soon became one of the largest and busiest hotels in the city. The well-liked owner combined an astute business sense with "good will toward man," accumulating enough money from his hotel to buy a large property on Mission Street. He built a big home there and indulged his passion for collecting art, plants, animals, and trinkets. Eventually, Woodward opened his home and four acres of grounds to the curious public.

What did they see? His zoo was the largest on the West Coast. He had four museums and an art gallery, along with the first aquarium in the West (and one of the first in the world), a large roller-skating rink, a shallow lake with a boat ride, an Edison phonograph machine, a restaurant, and a 5,000-seat pavilion for concerts. And just to keep people talking (as in word-of-mouth advertising), he employed a group of exotic Japanese acrobats, hired a tribe of Warm Spring Indians to camp on the property for a while, and featured a 19-pound, 25-inch-tall midget, called Admiral Dot, who, at the time, was 16 years old. He eventually grew to a height of 4 feet, putting the kibosh on his show biz career.

Visitors got all this for a 25-cent entrance fee (10 cents for kids). The fact that Woodward served no alcohol here either didn't seem to discourage people. Alas, after his death in 1879, the park faded, and, in 1893, Woodward's family divided it into 39 land parcels.

Of course, this is all very interesting background, but you're really here for the pie. And if you're not, you should be. It is outstanding. Rhubarb strawberry, the summer special, combines sweet and tart in layers that explode like little flavor bombs in your mouth—no gelatinous filler or overly sweetened ingredients. Likewise, the crust is exquisite: light and flaky as opposed to the soggy and slightly burned efforts common in the pie world. Pear sour cherry, apple cranberry, huckleberry, and peach are some of the other seasonal pies you must try.

Pastry chef Alan Carter is the gentle man behind the dough. After working in the financial services industry, he leapt into pastry making by enrolling at the California Culinary Academy (2002). Baking had been a hobby since childhood, when he learned the basics from his grandmother on her farm in Mississippi—he would wake up early and help her prepare the hearty main meal of the day. His dream had always been to open a bakery. His talent was obvious. Alan began working at Chow restaurant in San Francisco and soon became head pastry chef for all three Chow locations. He revamped their desserts and pies. The next step: a move to Paris where he studied under master pastry chefs (an apprenticeship of sorts). Back in San Francisco, he carefully folded what he had learned into his own recipes.

Then, it was time. Alan and co-owner Bill Clarke decided to open Mission Beach Café and build it, initially, around Alan's pastry. The amazing thing is that neither of them had done this before. Bill was in the classic modern furniture business for eighteen years—he owned various galleries and provided his clients with design work.

"I bought this building in 2003. And I found a commercial kitchen hidden behind one of the walls," said Bill. "I thought, that's for my best friend, Alan. Someday we'll do something with it." The previous owner had opened a café in the space toward the end of the dot-com boom; it closed six months later. Twenty years earlier, it was a corner grocery and then a wholesale Greek bakery.

"I had my furniture gallery here for about two years, in this dog-eared corner of the Mission," continued Bill. "It seemed like the neighborhood was changing rapidly. The projects came down and modern low-income housing went in, along with the beautiful Owen Kennerly townhouses across the street. Families with kids were moving in. I thought the area needed a place for folks to gather. So we just went for it, blindly, because we didn't have much experience.

"I love our crowd," said Bill. "We have Mission hipsters. We have lesbian and gay couples. We have older couples and families. Everyone feels comfortable here. People come in and want to see if our pie measures up to their recipe or their mom's recipe. It's great. It's a mixed bag. I love that. It makes it exciting. And we have these relationships we didn't have before."

The café's corner location has high ceilings and natural light that make you feel good. Bill describes the décor as classic California modern (with a pinch of 1950s), heavily influenced by Japanese-American George Nakashima (1905–1990), who said, "A tree is our most intimate contact with nature." This master craftsman used rich-grained hardwoods to create his distinctive furniture. While in Japan, Nakashima worked for Antonin Raymond, a Czech-born architect who collaborated with Frank Lloyd Wright on Tokyo's Imperial Hotel.

Wright would definitely approve of both the custom-made, tall, straight-backed chairs—and the unique tables. One single piece of bay laurel wood gave birth to all the tables along the back wall; the remainder came from another single plank. All have hand-carved butterfly joints.

The butterfly joint looks like a bowtie and holds each café table together across its seam so that the two halves seem to hover, but are still structurally sound. George Nakashima is famous for using the butterfly joint in his furniture. He preferred to work with an entire piece of wood, cracks and all—and the butterfly let him do that by connecting and stabilizing each plank.

"We spent a lot of time picking out the beautiful wood for the tables… and choosing the artwork, and fixtures and finishes. My good friend Michael Brennan helped us with the layout and metal work design—we couldn't have done it without him. The photography is by Sharon Risedorph. I focused on the details, furniture, and design. Our beach reference is the sand in the hourglass sconces on the wall. All these things feed you, like the hit you get from a great painting. So add the layer of food, and it becomes an even greater experience," said Bill.

Since one cannot live by pie alone, Mission Beach Café offers many other delectable dishes. They fall into the categories of coffee and pastry, lunch/brunch, and neighborhood fine dining.

Start your day with a cup of Blue Bottle coffee (yum, and also in this book) and assorted pastries. Go ahead, have a couple.

If you arrive mid-morning to mid-afternoon, move on to lunch/brunch. Choose from a list that includes the following—a Mission Beach egg sandwich with homemade English muffin, fried egg, mushrooms, white cheddar, caramelized onion, and roasted potatoes; the friends school lunch special: half sandwich of the day, salad or cup of soup; or the fish of the day, say, a petrale sole with celeriac puree, baby mustard greens, leeks, buerre blanc.

Weekend brunch is very popular. Here's why: wild mushroom eggs benedict with spinach, caramelized onions, and truffle mornay sauce; the short rib hash with sweet potatoes, apples, and butternut squash; or the much-in-demand MBC pancakes with fresh strawberries and bourbon syrup.

You should return later for your afternoon wedge of pie. In addition to seasonal fruit flavors, consider the chocolate pecan, banana butterscotch cream, or coconut raspberry cream. (You can also buy a whole pie.) Need a break from the pie? Cleanse your palate with a slab of mocha cheesecake or something seriously chocolate, such as a flourless chocolate tart with raspberry sauce, or the Brooklyn blackout cake, a chocolate cake that took its name from World War II blackout drills. Originally developed during this period by Ebinger's, a popular chain of Brooklyn bakeries, the cake vanished in the early 1970s when the chain closed.

One of the Mission Beach Café customers asked Allen to recreate this old favorite from her childhood. Many have tried to duplicate the scrumptious Brooklyn blackout cake—and where many have failed, Allen succeeded. The customer tasted the cake and said, "That's it."

Allen's *cannelé* is also "it." And once again, he has succeeded where many have failed. If you are familiar with this small, French fluted cake (from Bordeaux), you know how hard it is for a pastry chef to get it right. Start with a copper mold, coated on the inside with beeswax and honey. Pour the crepe batter (that includes butter, sugar, and dark rum) and cook for an hour and a half at 400 degrees. The *cannelé* ends up crunchy on the outside and tender on the inside. Allen's are perfect.

Legends surround the origin of the *cannelé*. Most of these stories concur that the first was baked by French nuns sometime before the French Revolution. Some go on to say that

the good sisters made the cakes with flour donated from cargo ships in port; others claim the egg yolks came from winemakers who used only the whites to clarify their wines.

Moving on to dinner, soft lighting turns the café into a glittering jewel box—your cue to try the puree of sunchoke soup, sprinkled with vanilla oil and Buddha's hand zest, or warm curly endive and purple potato salad. In the entrée department, some possibilities are rabbit pot pie with roasted winter vegetables, a Prather Ranch filet mignon or beach burger with aged gouda, caramelized onion, mushrooms, and Kennebec fries (on many local top ten burger lists), or a vegan specialty. But, you need to view the entire delectable dinner menu before you make a choice.

By the way, the 40,000-acre Prather Ranch sits on a high mountain butte near Mt. Shasta in Northern California. Its dry-aged, certified organic beef comes from fat and happy, grass-fed cattle, raised in a humane fashion.

The dinner menu began slowly," explained Bill. "We started a tasting menu and then had appetizers and wine at night, which evolved into a full menu about two months later. This is never where I expected we'd end up. We just kind of sat back and let it unfold. There was some chaos, but it is turning out well. I wanted the café to find its own way."

If you ask Bill what he does when not working, he'll just laugh. He hasn't been to his 400-acre ranch in Mendocino in eight months, and he used to go every weekend. In his pre–Mission Beach Café furniture gallery days, his work life was less hectic and, more or less, solitary. Now, as the general manager of Mission Beach Café, he has a very public daily existence, with eighteen employees. "Getting the right mix of people, philosophy of food, execution, and service—and coordinating it all—is wild. Like a theater production every night," he said. "And when it comes together, there is a great vibe in the room, like a dinner party with friends."

Okay, let's get it straight. Mission Beach is not another yuppie hangout. It's a comfy café by day, and more of an intimate restaurant by night. Sit on a stool at the counter, grab a table, or settle into the supple leather cushions of the long, sofa-like bench on the back wall. The neighborhood is classic Mission District—modern low-income housing, nice townhouses, and a porno house . . . all brushing elbows. A cup of local-roast Blue Bottle coffee and a slab of wonderful pie is a good icebreaker for your first date with this place. Mission Beach Café has its own philosophy: to create artisan food for the community from fresh, seasonal, local ingredients. Anyone interesting come in here besides you? Yes, multiplatinum and four-time Grammy Award–winning singer-songwriter Tracy Chapman shows up from time to time.

Ritual Coffee Roasters

1026 Valencia Street
(415) 641-1011
6AM–10PM, Monday to Friday
7AM–10PM, Saturday
7AM–9PM, Sunday
www.ritualroasters.com

*E*ileen Hassi, the proprietor of Ritual Coffee Roasters, is really into coffee, as you might expect. She wasn't, however, born this way—the coffee bug hijacked her along the roadway of life early on (which wasn't that long ago because she is only in her early 30s).

A Brown University graduate, Eileen managed a coffee shop in the basement of the Washington, DC bookstore, Politics and Prose, while at the same time considering a PhD in religious studies.

Coffee won out. "I fell in love with the business," said Eileen. "I liked the people/service component, the math component (the bookkeeping). And I liked the craft of making coffee."

Next, Eileen headed for the renowned java town of Seattle to learn more about coffee and began working for Torrefazione Italia. The company transferred her to San Francisco as a store manager in the Financial District, and she was shocked at the general quality of coffee in the City by the Bay.

"I had actually decided that I was going to open a coffee shop on Valencia Street before I left Seattle, before I had even seen Valencia Street, based on Dave Eggers's description of it at a reading of *A Heartbreaking Work of Staggering Genius*," Eileen says. Eggers's memoir tells the story of how he became the official guardian for his 8-year-old brother (at age 22). It was his first book, and a Pulitzer Prize finalist.

"He came to Seattle to do a book reading and talk about how he opened a tutoring center/Pirate Store. I wanted to be the coffee shop that serves all those writers hanging out down there. I used to say I was going to open up a coffee shop that was the center of the early 21st–century literary movement," continued Eileen.

The Pirate Store is part of 826 Valencia (down a few blocks from Ritual), a writing lab for young people that Eggers started in 2002. As "San Francisco's only independent pirate supply store," it sells Scurvy Begone Pills, Mermaid Repellant, spyglasses, pirate dice, and

other pirate necessities. All proceeds go to the 826 Valencia Writing Center. Look for the building with the clockwork illustration on the façade.

Eileen spent her weekends on Valencia Street looking for a one-story building where she could roast coffee. She found her current location—at the time, a furniture store—and gave the owner her card, saying if you ever leave, please call me.

She eventually got that call, and after looking for a year and nine months, she had her spot. "When I was building this place, I was doing the tiling and painting, and people would pop their heads in and ask, "What's this going to be?' I'd say a coffee shop and they'd reply, 'That's the last thing we need, another coffee shop.' I said, 'You don't understand. It's going to be different. The coffee is going to be better. The staff will be nicer. The environment cleaner,'" explained Eileen.

The naysayers included coffee industry friends in Seattle. They claimed that San Francisco would reject good coffee because Peets is the hometown roast of choice—in their opinion an over-roasted drip coffee quaffed with lots of cream to make it palatable. (Seattle is a medium-roast espresso town.) To these it-can't-be-done folks, Eileen countered that she thought if people were exposed to something better, they'd embrace it. Ritual Coffee Roasters opened in May 2005, and by the second week of business, there was a line out the door. The Seattle people were wrong.

"There were a lot of transplants from Seattle and Portland who were, like—finally, there's good coffee here. And they kind of spread the word among all the other transplants from cities with good coffee. Then people who lived in the neighborhood all their life and were never exposed to really good coffee would try us, and say, 'I don't know why, but this is better,'" said Eileen.

"Naming the business was one of the hardest steps. 'Ritual' is a word I use to explain why coffee means so much to me: most people drink coffee every day, like they brush their teeth, read the headlines, and make the bed. But there is something sacred in drinking coffee. No matter how often I do it, or how distracted I am, when I take the first sip of my coffee, I'm grateful to be drinking it—grateful for all the hands that went into making it and getting it to

me," continued Eileen. "On another level, for us obsessive types, there's something ritualistic in preparing it: each step is repeated, but always with intention."

Let's talk coffee beans for a minute. The species name for the original coffee plant is *Coffea arabica*, discovered in Ethiopia where it still grows wild. This plant likes warm climates, high altitudes, and volcanic soil. The better arabica, referred to as "hard bean," grows at altitudes of 3,000 to 4,500 feet. Higher up (above 4,500 feet), you'll find the really good stuff, called "strictly hard bean"— these beans mature slowly and become harder and denser than beans grown at lower levels. In general, the harder the arabica bean, the better the coffee.

On the other hand, *Coffea robusta (Coffea canefora)* is the bean of choice for the big commercial coffee producers. It is more resistant to disease and grows at lower altitudes where there is more rain and higher temperatures. Angola, Cameroon, and the Congo produce robusta. With this bean, you lose the flavor and aroma found in arabica, not to mention that the cheaper robusta beans can have 40 percent more caffeine. Many roasters of traditional Italian espresso use a pinch of robusta to make a thicker crema.

Before coffee leaves the country of origin, it has to be within a certain moisture range. If it's too low (below 9 percent), the beans absorb moisture from the surrounding environment, and from whatever shipboard cargo happens to be stored nearby, such as gasoline. If the beans are too wet (above 13 percent), they get moldy.

"Just last week, I smelled some of the green coffee that had just come from El Salvador, in a burlap sack. It was this year's crop, very fresh. And then I smelled some of the coffee from Colombia that's vacuum packaged in a box. The coffee from El Salvador smelled like green coffee, but it also kind of smelled like a burlap sack. And the vacuum-packed smelled like a starburst. It preserved all those natural flavors. So I'm predicting that soon we won't be buying coffee in plain burlap. Mostly, it will all be vacuum packed," said Eileen. (There is also an in-between solution: lining burlap sacks with gas and moisture-proof plastic bags called GrainPro SuperGrainbags. The majority of coffee now comes either vacuum-packed or in GrainPro bags.)

Eileen knows many of her suppliers in South America, Central America, and Brazil. There's Ruvaldo Delarisse from Chapadao de Ferro, Brazil, who produces her Sweet Tooth single-origin espresso; Alejandra Chacon and father Arturo, growers of Villalobos and Caturra coffee on their small farm 1750 meters above sea level in Tarrazu, Costa Rica; and Colombian microlots producers Edifonso Yara, Omar Viveros, and Hugo and Duver Rojas, delivering exceptional coffee from their tiny farms.

"Most of the farmers I've met said I was the first person they actually talked to that bought their coffee. I look forward to the day when I know the face of everyone I buy coffee from," said Eileen.

For fun, she travels to coffee-producing countries and visits coffee farms. She also likes to visit coffee shops. Eileen says, "All my hobbies have something to do with coffee. I took up scuba diving recently, but that was primarily in coffee producing countries: Guatemala, Costa Rica, and Panama."

Even though you start with good beans, it's possible to screw them up in the roasting process. Ritual did not roast their own beans in the beginning, but eventually they jumped in—and, as Eileen said, "It was trial and error... mostly error, but after a few months we rolled out some espresso which, in retrospect, was terrible. But we learned a lot." The company has been artfully roasting since 2006.

Ritual Coffee Roasters sells mostly single-origin (from one specific growing region), single-farm coffee. Espresso is their only blend, using two to four beans, and it changes seasonally depending on what's fresh. "This is uncommon," explained Eileen. "Let's say we decide this Brazilian coffee is outstanding. We add a Rwanda coffee to bring a little fruit and acidity to the flavor. When the Brazilian goes away, because it's not fresh or we're running out of it, we choose another coffee and build another blend around that. We don't have a standard house blend. Most roasters will say this is my espresso—it's chocolate and hazelnut, for example—and try to match that consistent flavor profile throughout the year."

Ritual's Director of Espresso, Ben Kaminsky, determines which coffee will become the next Sweet Tooth (single origin espresso of the month), and he also creates the seasonal espresso. The roastery—with an espresso machine solely for training and creating the espresso program—is a playground for people who love coffee. There is nearly always a cupping or tasting for either selection, quality control, or educational purposes—all of this so you can have that excellent shot of espresso.

The weakest link in the espresso chain is often the barista—an 18-year-old with a bad attitude who, in the course of making your cappuccino, burns the coffee and/or scalds the milk. Not so at Ritual Coffee Roasters. "We're trying to make it a career. The most important thing is that the people we hire really love coffee. Many have been baristas in other places, but if not, we're willing to teach them. First, they learn how to open and close the store, and work the register," explained Eileen.

"We're actually building a barista certification program where the baristas go through a series of tests and classes to become certified to work behind our bar. The first test is brewing coffee using a glass filter called a V-60, a siphon, and other brewers in our basement lab," she continued. "They learn how to clean the grinder burrs, then move on to taking care of the espresso machines. Learning how to make an espresso is the last part of their training."

So let's say you're an ace barista and you want to get out there and, you know, mix it up a little in the coffee world. What do you do? Well, you enter a competition called the United States Barista Championship (USBC), which describes itself as "an event designed to encourage and recognize professional achievement in the art of espresso beverage preparation and service." (That is, to elevate barista standards worldwide.) In the space of

15 minutes, you prepare four espressos, four cappuccinos, and four original signature drinks (no alcohol) for four judges.

It takes hundreds of hours of practice and clawing your way through regional competitions to become the national winner, representing the United States at the World Barista Championship (WBC). This is the big time, where you're up against top baristas from other countries. (The competition has grown from 25 to 56 nations since it started in 2000.) The drill for the WBC is the same, except that you must use the Nuova Simonelli espresso machine (and a coffee grinder of your choice). A head judge, four sensory judges, and two technical judges evaluate taste, cleanliness, creativity, technical skill, and overall presentation.

Italians don't seem to score at the WBC, even though Italy has the highest barista standards of any country. The norm in Italy is really good espresso (or caffè) because the Italians expect it. "The service is outstanding and the professionalism of the Italian bars is something to aspire to," said Eileen. Oddly

enough, when she brought her espresso to an international coffee conference, the Italians thought it too sweet, while the northern Europeans, English, and Australians loved it.

For many San Franciscans, Ritual's coffee moves the ground(s) under their feet. Something else would have done this about one hundred years ago, if you were in the area during the 1906 earthquake. The ground under the Valencia Hotel at 718 Valencia, between 18th and 19th (a few blocks down from Ritual Coffee Roaster's current location), both moved—and sank. Built on the filled-in Laguna de los Dolores (see the Mission Beach Café chapter), the four-story frame building disappeared into the soft, wet ground, drowning and crushing at least 15 people. Within 47 seconds, the fourth floor became the ground floor.

Whether you're a normal person or a card-carrying coffee nerd, this is the place for you. Notice the ever-changing menu with seasonal selections for both espresso and drip coffee, brewed to order. An obsession with quality goes into roasting every bean and pulling every shot. Outside, there's a big red flag with a coffee cup logo and revolutionary star (reminiscent of the hammer and sickle), and inside, a warm/warehouse feel and wi-fi. Clusters of single light bulbs hang from the ceiling to remind you of your "inner struggling artist in a garret." The coffee bar, a vintage 1919 Probat gas coffee roaster, and stacks of 132-pound burlap bags full of green coffee beans use to all inhabit the same room, but due to growing popularity and economies of scale, Ritual is now roasted in a nearby warehouse on Howard Street. As for food, owner Eileen Hassi's philosophy is "If I can pick it up with a pair of tongs and put it in a bag, I'm willing to sell it." Tracy Chapman sightings reported here. You'll find a Ritual outpost at Flora Grubb Gardens, 1634 Jerrold Street, in the Dogpatch area of the city, and in Napa at the Oxbow Public Market, 610 First Street.

La Copa Loca

3150 22nd Street (at Capp Street)
(415) 401-7424
1PM–9PM, Monday
9AM–10PM, Tuesday to Saturday
10AM–9PM, Sunday
www.lacopalocagelato.com

*M*any people say it's difficult to find good gelato outside Italy, and they're right. However—lucky for you—Mauro Pislor, an upbeat young Italian, decided to open a gelato shop in the Mission District. He comes from *la provincia di Belluno* in Northern Italy, gelato central in a nation that has raised gelato making to an art form. *Gelatai* from this area of the Veneto have migrated to every corner of the world.

The migration began with the economic downturn of the late 1800s and continued into the 1920s. Many local farmers, miners, and artisans headed north to Vienna in the summer, selling roasted chestnuts, caramel apples, and pears—and eventually *gelato artigianale* (homemade ice cream). Around 1870, two Italians got the first license to make and sell gelato in Vienna.

The city of Belluno is one hour north of Venice by car. Above it, in the Dolomites near the Austrian border, sits the region of Cadore, home of Mauro's village, Peron di Sedico. He grew up on a farm near this mountain community of 300 people. According to Mauro, 60 of them are gelato makers. "They say there is always a Bellunese behind any great gelato," he said. The entire area (excluding Venice, which has lost almost all of its *gelato artigianale*) is peppered with great gelato places. "Cold, sun, rain—it doesn't matter. We eat gelato there," continued Mauro. "We only stop from December to February."

Mauro learned how to cook from his father, who at one time had his own seafood restaurant, and presently manages three restaurants on the Riviera della Versiglia (the Tuscan Riviera). "I thought he would be retired, enjoying life right now, but he gets bored staying at home," said Mauro, who started in his father's kitchen at age 13, and also learned the basics of *la cucina Veneta* from his mother, uncle, and grandmother.

Eventually, he became a chef like his dad, and after a stint at the Hyde Park Hotel in Knightsbridge, returned to Italy for his compulsory military duty. Following that, in 1992, Mauro was thinking of going back to London when an Italian friend, married to an American woman, asked him to help open a restaurant in San Francisco. So he came to the City by the Bay.

The first gelato maker in the family, Mauro had dreamed of opening a gelateria since he was a kid. He finally decided to make his move in San Francisco because "there was no good gelato in town." A schoolmate, whose dad was a *gelataio* for 40 years, owned a gelateria in Germany—Mauro trained there for a week. "I saw how he was doing it. I liked his quality. When I came back, I worked here in restaurants for another couple years, and then I opened this place," said Mauro.

He scouted locations for six or seven months, but kept coming back to the corner of 22nd and Capp—a vacant coffee shop, owned by the guy in the check-cashing shop next door. Mauro lives only three blocks away and knew this as a spot with drug dealing and prostitution, yet he saw its potential. He decided to rent the space and take a chance. It worked—the presence of his gelateria helped clean up the corner.

In June of 2005, Mauro opened an Italian gelateria with a Spanish name—*La Copa Loca* or "crazy cup." He thought the name sounded exotic. "In my original business plan, I had 30 seats with beer, wine, and a bar. And then I got scared. I decided to try the small place to see

if people like it. Eventually, I may expand," Mauro explained.

He makes his own base everyday—which means he mixes fresh milk, cream, and sugar; brings the liquid up to 85°C; lowers it to 5°C; and lets it sit. (According to Mauro, some gelato makers in Europe still use eggs as a coagulant, but that is a risk for salmonella.) The next step is to add the flavoring—fresh fruit or imported Italian flavors—and put this mixture in the batch freezer (a giant freestanding mixer). In 8 to 10 minutes, you have gelato.

"I keep the gelato about two days, some flavors a little longer. I have only 24 flavors on display, and I keep some soy and some sugar-free in the back," Mauro said. "The ingredients are all good, and I make small batches, three liters at a time. My concept was to keep a lower price. In that way, I do much more volume... and I'm able to keep it fresh. I have people who come here almost every day, and they say, 'We're never going back to ice cream.'"

What's the difference between ice cream and gelato, you ask? To begin with, gelato has less butter fat—about 5 to 8 percent, compared with ice cream at 10 percent (for low-end commercial) up to 16 percent (for the really good stuff). Also, gelato is denser than ice cream, which has more air content or "overrun" as they call it in the trade. The more air you add to a batch, the higher the yield. Mauro says his overrun is only about 30 percent, whereas with some ice creams it is 100 percent, which doubles the size of a batch. Finally, the serving temperature of gelato is higher than that of ice cream. That is to say, your cup of gelato arrives slightly warmer and softer than your ice cream cone.

For his water-based *sorbetto* (sorbet), Mauro mixes fresh fruit with water and sugar, and then adds a little stabilizer such as guar gum, which, he says, "holds things together. In the summer I barely use stabilizer, because it's warmer and you don't need it."

Mauro's best salespeople are his customers—60 percent Latino. They often bring a friend (and first timer), explaining all the flavors and what's really good. "Sometimes, I don't have to do anything. They just sell it for me. That's a nice feeling," said Mauro.

He employs three Latino workers, and this confuses some people—especially the Italian customers who assume, because the gelateria has a Spanish name, that his workers own it and he scoops gelato for them.

Mauro has certainly immersed himself in the neighborhood—he lives nearby and is married to a Latina, Sandra. She was raised in Mexico City by her Spanish dad and American mom, until age six, when the family moved to Stockton. Mauro and Sandra have a baby boy, Alessio, and another child on the way.

His workday runs from 7AM to 8PM; Sunday is his day off with the family (sometimes). For fun, he used to camp, hike, ski, snowboard, and, in Italy, race bicycles. "Also, I have a motorcycle, like any good Italian. But I don't have a Ducati... yet. Maybe after selling one million scoops," said Mauro. His wife likes his gelato, but is not too happy about the motorcycle.

Mauro tells the story of a former girlfriend, who didn't make the cut, more or less, because of gelato. "Seven years ago, I took my girlfriend to Italy, to the best gelato place in my town—Il Gelato. I was all excited. And she said, 'What's the big deal?' Wow, she couldn't tell the difference. It shocked me. Oh my god, you have no idea. We're done here. Take a plane back. Leave now. And that's why I broke up with her. It was no different than regular American ice cream for her," exclaimed Mauro jokingly (but not really).

"Il Gelato has a line every day during the summer. In the winter, people drive there and beg them to open. 'No, another two weeks. It's too cold,' they say. I went back in January and they weren't open. One day the sun came out—it was a nice 20 degrees. So they opened up with eight flavors. I had Sicilian pistachio, and it was incredible. People pulled up and stopped," he continued. "It's on the way to the airport. I even changed my flight, so I could get their gelato. I used to leave at 6AM. Now I always leave at 10 and stop by to get my last gelato before I leave.

"When I'm home, I eat gelato every day. Either I go down to the gelateria, or my grandmother has it at home. She's 96 and still sharp. I used to help my grandfather on the farm, out in the field. I'd also take the sheep to the pasture and clean the horse stable. My grandfather used to kill the pigs and make salami. The farm's gone now—I'd give everything for a week back there," said Mauro, an only child and the only family member in the United States.

He's serious about his gelato and precise with the ingredients. (In fact, his favorite instrument is the scale.) He likes everything exact at home, too. His wife always weighs the pasta servings—150 grams for the two of them. "Maybe it's because I'm a Virgo and they're very picky."

If you're also serious and picky about gelato, then La Copa Loca is the place for you. "Nobody makes sundaes like I do," claims Mauro. His various signature sundaes (very labor intensive), resemble the following: a snow man, a bumblebee, Pinocchio, a pizza, a dish of spaghetti carbonara, and of course, this being the Mission—a taco and a burrito. There are also the classics: a banana split and a straight-up chocolate sundae. For something simple, go for a cup of his *variegato all'amarena* (chunks of sour black cherry in vanilla gelato). It's as good as the pistachio, the *stracciatella* (shavings of chocolate and cream gelato), and the passion fruit and blood orange sorbets.

It's called La Copa Loca, "the crazy cup" in Spanish, though since owner Mauro Pislor is Italian it should be called La Coppa Pazza. But nevermind, his gelato is great. And his fun, odd-ball animal-and food-shape sundaes are definitely pazza and tasty. (He also serves crepes and panini.) Mauro opened the place because he couldn't find good gelato in San Francisco. Now he wants to be gelataio to the people—offering really good quality and affordable prices. Scared of the Mission? Don't be, he says. Like most places, the neighborhood is fine unless you look for trouble.

Philz Coffee

3101 24th Street (at Folsom Street)
(415) 875-9370
6AM–8:30PM, Monday to Friday
7AM–8:30PM, Saturday & Sunday
www.philzcoffee.com

When Phil Jaber was young, his dad said, "Son, if you want to be a good merchant and have lots of friends, build a church everywhere you go."

"What are you talking about, dad? There's a church down the street," answered Phil.

"No, you dummy. Build a church means make a friend. Be sincere and honest with him like you are at church. Treat people like you want to be treated. Don't cheat, steal, or lie."

From the looks of things, Phil, the owner of Philz Coffee, followed his dad's advice. Clearly, his customers like him, and he greets many by name as they enter his shop. (He's the guy with the spectacles and signature fedora.)

"Philz is one of the main reasons I get up in the morning. Sometimes it's the only reason," writes one diehard on Yelp, the popular user reviews and recommendations website. Phil sees it this way, "I'll tell you straight up, the best clientele in the country come to Philz coffee shop. They are beautiful, smart, intelligent—no drama."

The coffee shop opened in 1972 as Gateway Market, a corner store selling food, ice cream, sandwiches, liquor, and cigarettes. Phil sold the liquor and cigarettes at a discount. "I come from the old school," he says. "I'd say to a customer, 'How much do you pay for Johnny Walker, 20 dollars? For you, 15 dollars, but keep it to yourself.' People like to talk about good things, that's why I tell them keep it to yourself. I never charged one more than the other. For many years I did that, and built a clientele."

Phil was born in Ramallah, part of the West Bank. He grew up in a small village of seven families located about 15 minutes north of Jerusalem. His family left the Middle East in 1967 just before the Six-Day War and lived in Amsterdam, Canada, and Texas before coming to California. "I never went back. My family goes back and forth. We still have our house there. Maybe soon, I'll go back," he said. The compound where his extended family lived includes a two-story house, closed for 40 years, and in front of that, a three-story rental house.

When his mother and grandmother used to sit around and drink Arabic coffee, Phil would sneak a little cup of his own. The first time, he burned his mouth. As he became older and wiser (at age 6), he put ice in the coffee. "I always liked coffee when I was a little kid," Phil explained. "I was born to make coffee."

Phil's interest in coffee grew. At the age of 15, his family lived in Emeryville, and he worked a few hours a day for an old Italian who taught him a lot about the coffee business.

Later on, in the Gateway Market, Phil set up a little coffee lab, but he never sold to the public. He was always experimenting, perfecting his brew. For 25 years, he took coffee seminars, visited coffee shops (1,100 total), and roasted coffee. Then, in 2003, Phil was ready.

He went home and told his wife, "I think I'm going to sell my coffee."

She said, "Why don't you sell the shop and just relax for a year?"

"No, I think I'm changing the shop, tomorrow."

"To what," she asked.

"To a coffee shop," he answered.

Phil called St. Anthony's where he knew a priest. "Father," he said, "I'm going to give you all the groceries in my shop. Can you send a truck over here?" It was $60,000 worth of inventory. Phil took the wine home and sold the liquor to a friend. Within two days, the store was empty, shelves of groceries replaced by funky couches and mismatched chairs—and after six months of struggle, Philz Coffee took off.

A great cuppa Joe doesn't come easy. A man has to have his guidelines, and Phil's overarching tenet is, "One cup at a time," as his tagline states. And no single-origin beans—he believes in blending anywhere from two to seven beans for each of his various coffees. Behind the counter sit eight single-serve drip stations. First, the cream goes in the cup, then the barista pours boiling water over the fresh coffee grounds resting in a paper filter. And drip, drip, drip, you have a handmade cup of Philz. (Phil does not believe in coffee machines, either—for him, the drip method releases the true flavor.)

Phil buys beans from a local roaster. "There is always someone who does things better than you. I found someone who is passionate about what he does, and I deal with him. I even give him more money. If he asks for a dollar, I say, 'No. A dollar twenty for you.'" In his unpretentious office—a 100-year-old food locker—Phil blends his coffee, counting out the various beans as if he's filling a prescription in a compounding pharmacy.

His fanatical following has a choice of a core group of flavors with quirky names (and don't ask, each blend is a secret). Here are some of them:

In the light roast department, Phil developed Greater Alarm in honor of the San Francisco Fire Department and its firefighters. Another popular light roast got its name from Phil's exclamation after first tasting it—Sooooo Good.

Smooth and full-bodied Aromatic Arabic gives you a dark roast coffee. Jacob's Wonderbar Brew, named after Phil's son, offers another dark roast with the flavor of nuts and chocolate.

Medium-roast Tesora was Phil's first blend, and seven years in the making (like a Cecil B. DeMille film in the mid-1950s). Try this for your first taste of Philz. And, then there's Philharmonic—it orchestrates a light Turkish coffee flavor with a harmonious layer of cardamom.

This might be a good time for some coffee Phil-osophy. According to Phil, "The important thing is how you play with coffee and how you touch it. It is very fragile.

"To me coffee is like medicine to your body, my friend. Coffee is good for you. It makes you patient. It makes you calm. Because the way you handle it, the way you sip it, the way you socialize with other people—coffee makes you relaxed, settled." He continued, "Oh, you would say coffee makes me wired. No, coffee doesn't do that. It's all in our head.

"How much do I like coffee—I'm into coffee like the Pope is into God."

Family is very important to Phil Jaber, and an integral part of the business. He met his wife, Hilda, while waiting in line to buy a ticket at a movie theater. He glanced over at her and lightning struck. Not being shy (as you'll notice when you meet him), Phil introduced himself. They've been married since 1980—"She's the best thing that ever happened to me," said Phil.

Phil and Hilda have two girls and a boy. Daughter Jessica helps run Philz Coffee. It was her idea to use the distinctive "z" in Philz Coffee. "She is very sharp, like a razor blade," said Phil proudly. Jacob, his 22-year-old son, also works in the business. He came to Phil after a year of college and said, "Dad, I'm not going to waste three more years. I want to make money with you." Younger daughter Gina attends the University of Southern California (USC), studying medicine.

"I want my kids to balance their lives," said Phil. He divides his day into three parts: 12 hours for work, 8 hours for sleep, and 5 hours for relaxation and family. If you noted this totals 25 hours, it's because Phil finds his day an hour or two on the short side. When he feels too much stress, he follows his grandfather's advice: "Lay down, take a deep breath, and say to yourself, 'Shut up and like it.'"

As Gateway Market morphed into Philz Coffee, the Mission District neighborhood around it also changed. A mix of Russians, Italians, and Mexicans predominated until the late 1970s and 1980s, when the Russians and Italians moved out and Latinos from El Salvador, Nicaragua, Honduras, and Colombia replaced them. "There were lots of families. Father, mother, children, grandparents all dressed nice, holding hands, going to church," explained Phil. "In the old days, people used to come around looking for a house to rent. Now it's all singles. They're looking for one room to rent. Look outside on the street—the average age is 25–30. Some young people come here, and I give them advice. I'm a father figure for them." One of the things he says is the following: "Forget and forgive, and never forget to forgive."

There's a mixed bag of customers in Philz, including computer nerds, Mission District hipsters, policemen, firemen, former San Francisco Mayor Gavin Newsom, and writer/director Quentin Tarantino, who dropped in once, evaluating his experience this way, "Philz mocha rules." You could also bump into George Maguire, a local actor and a Philz regular. He played a policeman in the Will Smith vehicle *Pursuit of Happyness* (2006), filmed in San Francisco.

Phil's favorite story involves a policeman: "I was driving, and all of a sudden, this motorcycle cop, a CHP (California Highway Patrolman), stopped me on the freeway. He came to the window, and I said, 'Officer, what seems to be the problem?'

He said, 'No problem. I saw your van said Philz Coffee, so I stopped you because I want to meet you. My wife is possessed with your coffee.'"

After you're sated with Philz coffee, visit nearby Balmy Alley. Stand in Philz doorway facing 24th Street, take a right and walk down a few blocks. This alleyway of art, inspired by WPA/Diego Rivera–style murals, runs between and parallel to Treat Avenue and Harrison Street. It started with a 1971 "community paint-in" and has grown to include Latino/Mission-themed murals on every wall, gate, and garage lining the alley. They run the gamut from the whimsical, such as a pink flamingo gas meter incorporated in a Frida Khalo mural, to expressions of outrage at US Policy in Central America.

One cup at a time—that's how they do it at Philz Coffee. Not to worry, you won't wait too long. And, anyway, it's worth the wait. Philz is friendly and funky, lots of regular and neighborhood folks. "Sometimes I come here just to be with the people," says owner Phil Jaber. The focus is on his specially blended drip coffee; consequently, the only eats are pastries. Start with medium-roast Tesora—seven years in the making, creamy smooth, and made by pretty girls. When you come into the shop, Phil wants you to feel comfortable like you just entered Grandma's. There are additional locations near AT&T Park (home of the San Francisco Giants), in San Francisco's Castro District, and at the Civic Center.

A bit off the beaten track, but not too far from downtown, these two neighborhoods are worth a visit. Both have done an amazing turnaround: Dogpatch going from rundown blue collar to vibrant and livable, and Mission Bay moving from urban desolate to rebuilt and rediscovered.

MISSION BAY / DOGPATCH

· 5 ·

Axis Café

1201 8th Street
(415) 437-2947
8AM–9PM, Monday to Friday
10AM–3PM, Saturday & Sunday
www.axis-cafe.com

*L*et's say you're sitting at one of the tables in Axis Café's outdoor patio, and have just finished a luscious bison burger, along with a bottle of tasty Sierra Nevada Pale Ale. And let's say you then decide to kick back and time travel, from that exact spot, to the year 1750. (This is 26 years before the arrival of explorer Juan Bautista de Anza and the Spanish Padres.) You would find yourself stuck in the muddy marsh at the edge of Mission Bay, a natural cove almost entirely filled in during the past 250 years. All that remains is a narrow channel that meets San Francisco Bay at an area called China Basin.

As you sink slowly into the mud, you'd have to contend with traffic, but not the vehicular type. Instead, most likely, you'd see Ohlone Indians navigating the waters in the *tule balsa*—a reed boat that looks like the offspring of a raft and a canoe. The Ohlone paddled around Mission Bay and up Mission Creek, which ran down from a lake called Laguna de Manantial (or Laguna de los Dolores). Later on, settlers used Mission Creek—40-feet wide at some places—to carry supplies in skiffs up to Mission Dolores, located near the lake's shore.

In San Francisco's early days, there was a lot of fresh free-flowing water along Islais, Lobos, and Mission creeks. And it's still flowing, although mostly underground or through sewer pipes. Natural springs from Mount Olympus and Eureka Valley feed Mission Creek, a major source of drinking water to San Francisco in its early days. The old Pepsi bottling plant, formerly located at 17th and Valencia, used this water for bottling operations until the 1990s, as did a large commercial laundry.

Another major water source, the subterranean Hayes River, flows about 15 feet below the surface, originating near the Lone Mountain area and emptying into Mission Bay. In the old days, many landowners in the Hayes River's path drew well water from it. Some places still get their water from the Hayes—such as the California Automobile Association, the Fillmore Center, and the public fountains at the United Nations Plaza. The Powell Street BART station and city government buildings at Civic Center also draw Hayes water—albeit not by choice. Their pumps run 24 hours to keep basements and tracks from flooding.

These millions of drinkable gallons flowing through San Francisco's city limits form the Mission Creek watershed (or drainage basin). The irony here: all this potable water goes down the drain, while the City imports water from the Hetch Hetchy Reservoir, 165 miles away. Back on dry land(fill), Axis Café sits at the cusp of Potrero Hill and the Mission Bay area of SoMa (South of Market). Formerly an industrial wasteland, this section features a

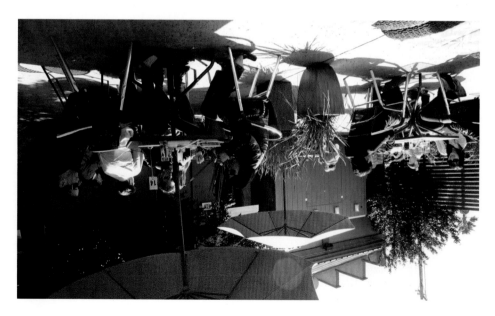

new 57.5-acre University of California San Francisco (UCSF) biomedical research campus, bioresearch firms, 6,000 condo units, a primary school, a new public library branch, and 48 acres of parks.

In this burgeoning neighborhood, an Aussie couple named Mark and Gail Smallcombe (joined by three enterprising locals: Nita Orozco, Mike Hardwick, and Nick Bovis) started the hip, unpretentious Axis Café. The kernel of the idea first came to Mark and Gail while they were on a beach in Indonesia, aptly named Dream Beach. Mark had thought about coming to the Bay Area for many years. "My first American friend in Australia was from San Francisco, and he would talk about surfing under the Golden Gate Bridge. He was 21, and I was 21. He was the guy who taught me to ski and introduced me to some adventures I never had before. And I was intrigued about San Francisco. It just happened that the forces of life drew us here—my wife and I don't have children, so it was fairly easy for us to relocate," explained Mark, an upbeat, energetic man who, at one time, developed numerous, large-scale community projects, along with a drug and alcohol rehabilitation center, in Newcastle, Australia.

He was initially invited to San Francisco in 2001 to launch a "C3" Church (Christian City Church), part of an international church movement that originated 30 years ago in Sydney. The café remained in the background until Mark introduced his idea to interior designer Nita Orozco and businessman Mike Hardwick. "I shared the vision of what he was trying to do. It intrigued me, and I decided to get involved," said Mike.

That vision: To create a living room for the community—where people can hang out, feel comfortable, and connect with others. All profits go to supporting the Axis Community Project, which provides programs and activities for neighborhood families.

Mark (now a permanent and happy resident of Potrero Hill) describes himself as an ordinary guy "with an extraordinary vision. And this kind of vision needs extraordinary people to help make it happen."

Their café required a home, and after a long search, they zeroed in on their current space. It was stand-alone (the café would host events, have live music, and make a bit of noise), and offered a great location with plenty of parking. The only problem—a wholesale furniture outlet was renting the building.

"It was all closed up. I knocked on the door," said Mark, "and out of the dark comes this guy all bleary eyed and says, 'What do you want?'

"'You might think this unusual, but have you thought about relocating? I'm interested in seeing if this place is available,' came the answer.

"'My god, how did you know?' asked the guy. 'I'm really in a situation right now where I can't afford the space. I'm looking for an out, and I don't know what to do.'"

Mark, Nita, and Mike shared their vision of the community café with the building's owner, Nibbi Brothers General Contractors, who loved the concept, and relocated the tenant to a smaller space, relieving him of his financial problem. Axis Café rented the building at an affordable discount. Everyone benefited. "It pays to knock on the door," said Australian Mark.

Italian-born carpenter Marino Nibbi first set up shop south of Market in 1950. One small job led to another and the excellence of his work propelled the business forward. To meet increased demand, his brother Pete joined him, and from there, Nibbi Brothers expanded dramatically to large construction projects. Mark feels that the company still has the soul of the original small family business. (The Nibbi's original cabinet shop is a couple blocks away.)

Originally a Chevron garage built around 1910, the building needed lots of work. The hoist bar used to lift engines out of trucks is still in the café, as is the mechanics pit, now covered by the stage.

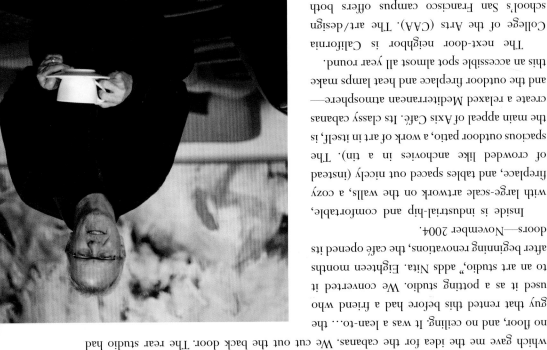

Big oil depots populated parts of nearby Potrero Hill in those days. "The construction is very interesting," said Mike Hardwick. "The walls are made from concrete and chards of pottery. You can actually walk under the building—there's water at high tide."

Nita Orozco created the feeling of Axis Café. "I thought all of the bones were there—all the key elements as far as what it could look like. It just needed to evolve. You go into a space before it's renovated, and you ask it what it wants to be. I think this is what this space wanted to be. It's much happier this way," she explained.

"In back, there was a huge mound of dirt and an old shed infested with feral cats, which gave me the idea for the cabanas. We cut out the back door. The rear studio had no floor, and no ceiling. It was a lean-to... the guy that rented this before had a friend who used it as a potting studio. We converted it to an art studio," adds Nita. Eighteen months after beginning renovations, the café opened its doors—November 2004.

Inside is industrial-hip and comfortable, with large-scale artwork on the walls, a cozy fireplace, and tables spaced out nicely (instead of crowded like anchovies in a tin). The spacious outdoor patio, a work of art in itself, is the main appeal of Axis Café. Its classy cabanas create a relaxed Mediterranean atmosphere—and the outdoor fireplace and heat lamps make this an accessible spot almost all year round.

The next-door neighbor is California College of the Arts (CAA). The art/design school's San Francisco campus offers both graduate and undergraduate programs in architecture and design, while its four-acre Oakland campus features undergraduate programs in art. Axis gives CCA student discounts and keeps track of exam schedules so the staff can be extra nice during midterms and finals.

The California Culinary Academy (right down the road) sends interns to the café's kitchen, which is run by Linda Edson. No slouch, she was a line cook at Gary Danko, in addition to working at Masa's and The French Laundry. "I never thought I'd work at a café. I really love fine dining—that was my passion. And I was never a prep cook. In fine dining, you charge a lot more and work with finer ingredients. There's more time to prep everything. So coming here, the challenge was to make good food fast," she said. "I planned to go work in Europe, and I had all these five-year plans, but I came here and I love what it stands for."

Much has changed since Linda started. At first, the café offered more quick meals—and then, eventually, expanded into serving breakfast, lunch, and dinner. The menu is based on her background growing up in Buenos Aires and her French/California culinary training, along with lots of fresh organic ingredients.

"I never grew up with American food—so I really don't like pizza, burgers, or fries, or hot dogs," explained Linda. "We had fresh milk and baked our own bread. My mother, who's French, was this huge health person." Linda has passports from three countries: France, Argentina, and the United States. She is also trilingual, as opposed to Mark, who jokes that he's bilingual: English and Strine, as in "g'day" and "owyagoin." (Strine is pretty much like English, except when you speak, you move your lips as little as possible. But rest assured, Mark moves his lips a lot for an Australian, so you'll understand him just fine.)

Linda's skirt steak in *filone* with arugula and vidalia onion will make you happy—as will the Thai snapper with cherry tomato and rice; the sweet potato ravioli with gorgonzola, rainbow chard, and broccolini; ahi tuna salad; fish tacos; and the (50 percent-less-cholesterol-than-beef) bison burger. They also make all their own pastries—just point, and you can't go wrong.

While everyone at Axis is proud of their food, they're most proud of the Axis Community Projects (ACP). "We are a nonprofit," explained Hannah Walker, director of ACP programs

and former primary school teacher in the UK. "All our profit goes to these projects—we provide activities, events, and programs for the community."

Here are some of the community-centered projects sponsored by Axis:

A moms' and toddlers' group called Little Angels meets every Tuesday from 2 to 4:30PM. Moms also run their own childcare co-op called Slippery Fish.

ACP art groups include Art Attack, an after-school art program for 3-to-6-year-olds; Family Art Night; and Door to My Future, a special project, involving 17 kids (with less than privileged backgrounds) from Potrero Hill. They began with a plain door as a canvas, which they filled with words and pictures representing their dreams and ambitions. The doors were displayed in Axis Café and at Soma Art Gallery. "We saw these kids blossom in just an amazing way," said Hannah Walker.

Most people who work in the café are under 30, and they're all given lots of opportunities. An example of this is Jennifer Bardellini, special events coordinator. She started at Axis as a waitress. "They believed in me, and came to me and said we need someone to take over events and marketing," she explained. "So I sat down and talked about what was needed—someone to try to get Axis out there."

Hannah Walker adds, "Jen just came in, and you could tell she was just going to own the events area. She had the gift for organizing."

"My whole career outlook completely changed because of this job. I love marketing, planning events, working with vendors, and writing up contracts," continued Jennifer.

Axis Café and Jennifer (with new events person Karina Paz) handle weddings, bar mitzvahs, book signings, corporate workshops—and events such as Renew Year's Eve, a huge party that raises money for Huckleberry House (a homeless teenagers' residence).

As for throwing a huge party, Axis Café offers an almost-anything-goes space that has been used to create a Las Vegas evening with a stage, slot machines, acrobats hanging from the main beam, monkeys out in back, camels out in front, and searchlights. There have also been carnivals, crazy weddings, and other over-the-top events.

The hugely popular *Ask a Scientist* lecture series is a monthly event—often with 200 people in attendance and a live video projection screen on the patio for latecomers. The series features scientific experts who give presentations and take questions. The topics vary from "Sex and War" to "The Science of How to Hit a Homerun."

This kind of intellectual stimulation fits in with the purpose of Axis, explained Mark. "We want to promote the transfer of ideas, like in the coffee houses of the beatnik era in San Francisco. We're not trying to promote a movement. We're just trying to provide an atmosphere for the exchange and connection." Hence, the name—Axis, as in a hub or point of connection.

The website says: "Food. Coffee. Art. Life." You can add: nice people, cool place to hang out, live music on some Wednesday and Friday nights. Former Mayor Willie Brown sent a nice letter for the grand opening. Former Police Chief Heather Fong drops by, and Animation Director Andrew Stanton (Academy Award–winner for Finding Nemo and WALL·E) had a kid's birthday party here. Once, German tourists showed up with a GPS system and no English—Axis had been mentioned in a German tourist magazine. But mostly, the café is looking for people like you.

Piccino Café & Coffee Bar

Corner of 22nd Street and Minnesota Street
(415) 824-4224

Café
11AM–9:30PM, Tuesday to Friday
10AM–9:30PM, Saturday & Sunday
Closed Monday

Coffee Bar
7AM–5PM, Monday to Friday
8AM–5PM, Saturday & Sunday
www.piccinocafe.com

Some people think they're sisters. In fact, they didn't even know each other that well when they opened Piccino Café in December 2006. "I guess we're kind of crazy," says Sher Rogat, the shorter of the two, with the pretty blue eyes. She and her charming co-owner Margherita Sagan jumped into things (more or less).

They met through mutual friends, and then kept running into each other at their favorite pizza and coffee places. It wasn't long before the two home cooks discovered they saw eye to eye on good food. At one point, they learned that a small commercial space in the Dogpatch neighborhood had become available. "Margherita wanted to open a café, and I wanted to do something on my own," explained Sher. "We saw the space and said, 'It's the perfect size.' The neighborhood was about to grow, and, at the time we opened, it didn't have a center. This corner felt like it was the center, in and of itself."

Their backgrounds are varied: Sher earned a Masters in Museum Studies and worked at Williams-Sonoma and Levi's, while Margherita got an MBA, started a food specialty business, worked in the corporate world, and taught business at San Francisco State University. In 2005, they decided to make the move. Neither had experience running a café, although both came from families of good cooks.

At the family home in Lucca, Italy, Margherita's mother baked bread every week in a wood-burning brick oven and grew most of the things they ate. "I learned some incredible things from her. Not an array of grandiose plans and meals, but a sensibility about the ingredients and how to handle them and combine them. I wish she were alive today. I really miss her, and her seeing this. She would have been very proud of me," said Margherita.

"Sher is good with the baking. Even before we opened, she was baking things in my tradition—desserts that are not overly sweet... not rich... but rustic and satisfying. You taste a single ingredient—like almond cookies, where you have that wonderful full taste of almonds. It's not dispersed into a sugary sweet," continued Margherita. "I haven't cultivated that side as much—for me, it's more the savory soups and pizza."

Sher grew up in Des Moines, Iowa, and attended high school in Portland, Oregon. Her father ran a Jewish community home for the elderly. She says, "All I wanted to do was hang out with the ladies in the kitchen. And my mother was a very good cook." She remembers her Franco-Prussian grandmother making braids of strudel on her nine-foot-long dining-room table.

The concept behind Piccino, according to both women, was to offer extraordinary pizza, tasty main courses, and light salads, along with a great coffee bar and baked goods. In other words, they transferred what they liked to do at home to a retail setting.

The secret behind their success is a focus on simple dishes made from local ingredients, purchased, as much as possible, directly from local producers: Fatted Calf Charcuterie, organic Mariquita Farm, Cow Girl Creamery, Star Route Farms, Dirty Girl Produce, Marin Sun Farms, and County Line Harvest.

Sher and Margherita have created a small simple menu. Start your day with a housemade pastry or a bowl of yogurt, fresh fruit, and Piccino granola. And don't worry about the barista screwing up your cappuccino—this guy (Brian) really knows what he's doing. Piccino uses its own special blend of Blue Bottle coffee.

For lunch, get into a pizza, especially if you like the wafer-thin Roman style. Order a traditional margherita (fresh mozzarella and tomato sauce) or the offbeat-and-tasty black mission fig, pancetta, balsamic, and mint pizza. Count on the salads to please your palate—an example is the seasonal wild arugula with strawberries, tarragon, and ricotta. The soups are also special—standouts being the *pappa al pomodoro* (a Tuscan tomato soup thickened with bread) and the carrot/leek.

The dinner menu has many of these same offerings along with some main dishes that change with the seasons. Two yummy examples are pancetta-wrapped quail with carnaroli rice stuffing and *broccoli di ciccio*, and Margherita's pork/beef polpette with soft polenta and tomato sauce. Pair this food with a selection from their straightforward and reasonable-priced vino.

And by all means, do not leave without sampling a slice of Sher's lemon tart. If you don't, it may result in a fine by the pastry police for extremely bad judgment. (Same goes for the new chocolate torta with crème Chantilly.)

So how is it going for these two ladies—given that jumping into a business partnership can be treacherous?

"Even though there are growing pains and sometimes we get on each other's nerves, we always come back to the fundamental truth that we like and respect each other very much," said Margherita. "Since opening, we've become very solid, and we've had challenges, but it's like there is an underlying bond of sisterhood that is keeping us at it."

"I like it when people think we're sisters. Because I think that in another life we were," adds Sher.

Margherita picks up on this: "I knew she was an Italian in another life, because she wouldn't have that sense of food, the essence of what's Italian—good ingredients, simply made dishes. It's not about suffocating the ingredients, but letting them shine."

Piccino Café's first home, at the corner of 22nd and Tennessee streets, was originally a grocery store when Italians filled the area. During the first half of 2011, the café moved one block up, to the corner of 22nd and Minnesota and a new home in a larger, completely restored, 150-year-old yellow building that oozes character. Here, Piccino accommodates 70 diners inside and another 35 outdoors on a quiet, sunny sidewalk. It continues to live roughly in the center of the nine-square-block Dogpatch neighborhood, a rectangle defined by 23rd Street, Highway 280, Mariposa Street, and Illinois Street.

In the early days, the Franciscan friars grazed cattle from Mission Dolores (established in 1776) here on the bayside flats of Dogpatch. The pastureland was later given to the sons of Francisco de Haro, the first mayor of Yerba Buena, and became part of the family's cattle ranch.

After the gold rush, industry arrived, and by the late 1860s, so did English, Scottish, and Irish immigrant workers, who, along with Italians, Scandinavians, and others, established the Dogpatch neighborhood. They found work at the central waterfront and in businesses such as the California Barrel Company, California Sugar Refinery, and the Atlas Iron Works. The 1865 construction of Long Bridge, a wooden causeway across the tidal flats of Mission Bay (following the path of today's 3rd Street), accelerated industrial development.

In the early 1870s, two railroads (the Southern Pacific and the Atchison, Topeka and Santa Fe) bought most of the land under Mission Bay, and began landfill and development projects. Railroad facilities, machine shops, industrial buildings, and workers' homes sprang up. Union Ironworks (started in 1849) moved from south of Market Street to Potrero Point in 1883, and by 1890, it employed half of Dogpatch's male adults, and soon became the West Coast's largest shipbuilder.

Of course, what you really want to know is—how did this area get that strange name? The story begins with Butchertown. By 1877, all of San Francisco's odiferous slaughterhouses had relocated to Bayview (down the road from Dogpatch) in order to be well away from the city center. Tallow works, tanneries, and fertilizer plants soon followed, and the neighborhood got the nickname Butchertown.

In Butchertown, it was common to see cowboys driving cattle from the railroad stockyards, at the west edge of Butchertown, to the slaughterhouses on the northeast. (This continued into the 1920s.) Stories circulate among old timers about cowboys running cattle down 3rd Street and sometimes riding up on the sidewalks to put themselves and their horses between pedestrians and rambunctious steers.

All slaughterhouses sat on pilings over the water so that Islais Creek and the bay's tides could disperse offal and manure. Sometimes the creek ran red with blood from butchered cows, and the occasional body part would wash ashore. These delicacies, along with scraps of meat discarded by the slaughterhouse, drew packs of feral dogs living in the area now referred to as Dogpatch. The very last slaughterhouse closed in 1971.

Today's Dogpatch gives you a good glimpse into the Dogpatch of 100 years ago, mainly because Mission Bay marshlands buffeted the area from the devastating fire that followed the 1906 earthquake. You'll see many old and historic buildings built between the 1860s and 1910—such as early 1880s Victorian houses on Tennessee and Minnesota streets, between 22nd and 23rd; three-story Irving M. Scott School, an 1895 structure (SF's oldest existing schoolhouse) at 1060 Tennessee, named after the owner of the nearby Union Iron Works shipyard; and the city's oldest firehouse at 1009 Tennessee, built in the late 1890s.

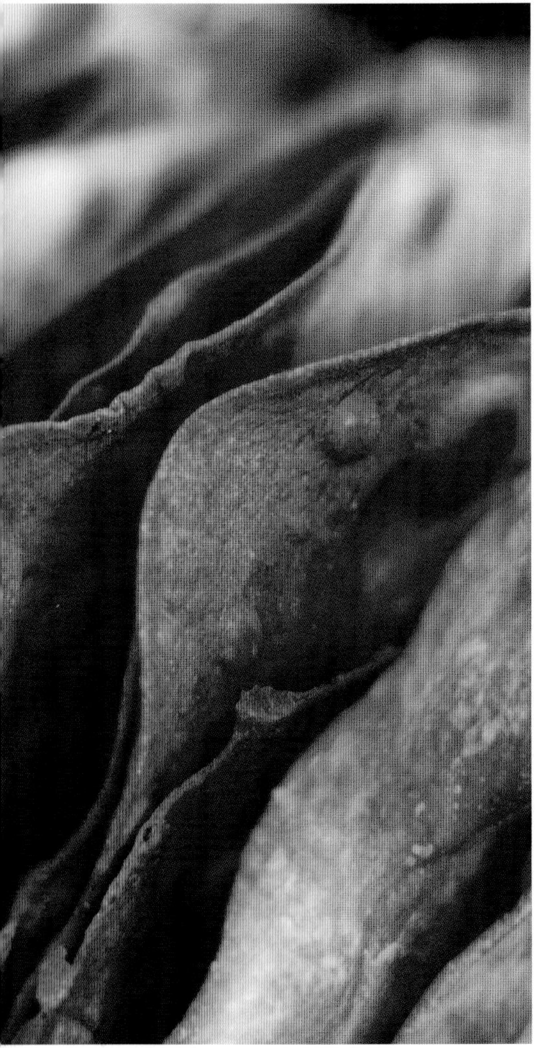

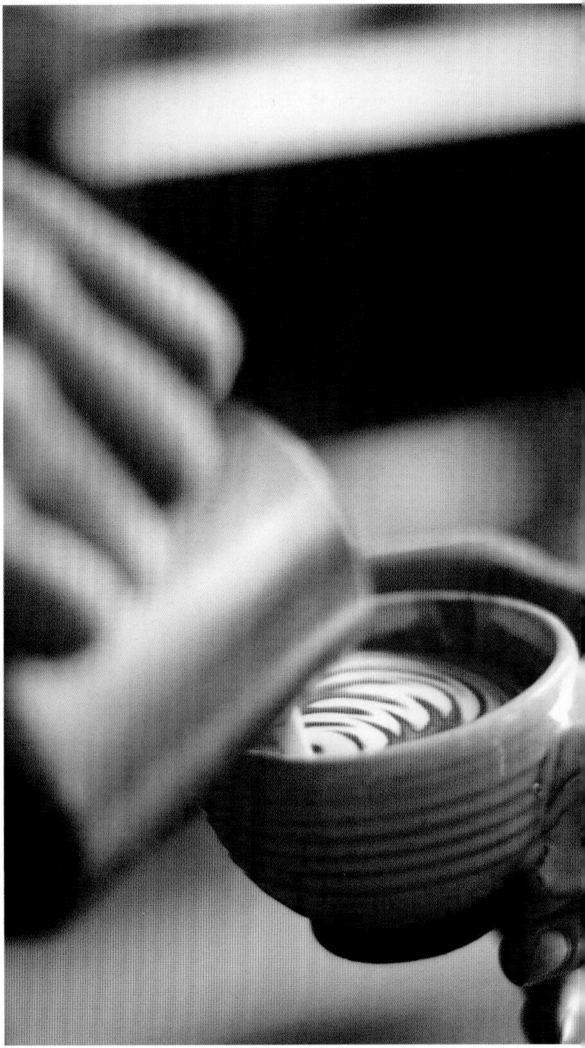

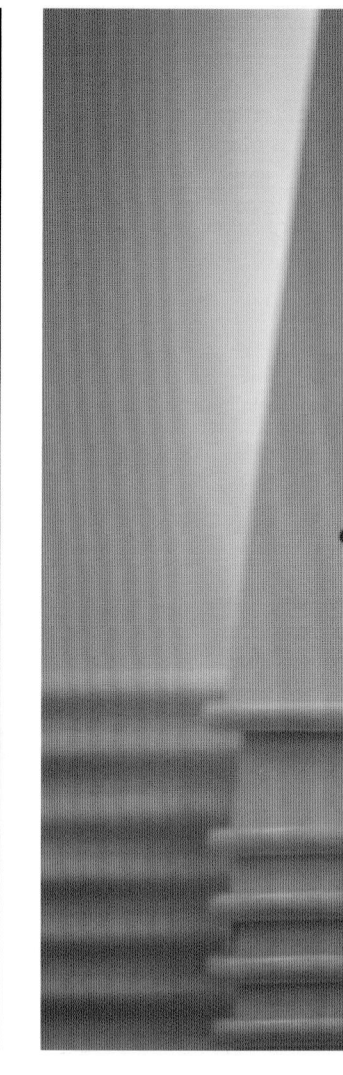

You'll also find a mix of heavy industry, light industry, artsy-type business (multimedia/ film studios, artists, photographers, graphic designers, and architects), restaurants, and the headquarters for the San Francisco Chapter of the Hells Angels. Not to worry about the latter, they're not interested in you, and pretty much keep to themselves, except for the occasional revving of Harley engines and blasting off to here or there. Their logo is a death's head with wings and the words "Hells Angels, Frisco." Nobody who lives in San Francisco calls it "Frisco" anymore, because it just isn't cool. (The Hells Angels, though, can call San Francisco pretty much anything they want.)

The core of Piccino's customers comes from the immediate neighborhood. Locals supported the place from the get-go, in spite of the fact that when it first opened, "there were so many screw ups with the orders that we gave free coffee to everyone," explained Sher.

"If we opened in any other area of the city, it would have been, 'Oh, another café.' But here," said Margherita, "they love us. For whatever reason, they're happy we're here, and show us in so many ways." For example, one neighbor brings popsicles on San Francisco's few sweltering days. Another regularly drops off a case of lemons, along with other produce from the garden. Moms, who visited regularly when pregnant, return often with their babies.

These two ladies do what they love, and it's working.

The Italian word piccino means "small and endearing," as in something you'd call your baby. Come in the AM for an excellent cappuccino or espresso (not burnt, not scalded, not bitter). Sit outside at night and enjoy a tasty, simple selection from the menu: a white pizza with fresh anchovies, agretti (a tart, salty herb), and preserved lemon; or sautéed white shrimp and roasted asparagus. This is a bright little corner of the world. And if it's good enough for singer/songwriter Tracy Chapman, celebrity chef Paul Bertolli, formerly of Oliveto and now head of Fra' Mani Salumi, and the-lesser-known-but-just-as-colorful residents of Dogpatch, it's certainly good enough for you.

· 6 ·

OUTSIDE THE CITY

*Y*ou'll probably cross the Golden Gate Bridge and travel through beautiful Marin County on your way to the wine country. Here are some gelato and pastry stopovers for you in Mill Valley, Larkspur, and San Rafael—*as if you haven't had enough to eat and drink already.*

noci

17 East Blithedale Avenue
Mill Valley
(415) 388-2423
11:30AM–9PM, Sunday to Thursday
11:30AM–10PM, Friday & Saturday
www.nocigelato.com

W hat's a young man to do if he decides, one day, to make *gelato artigianale* in the United States, where gelato is not a tradition and not even very well known? Do what Michael Orlandi did—find a partner and a good gelato school.

While traveling in Italy, Michael noticed the plethora of marvelous gelato and reflected on the absence of this high-quality product at home. (In case you're not sure, gelato is the Italian version of ice cream: denser, less air, richer tasting, and, believe it or not, with less butterfat than American-style ice cream).

The idea for gelateria Noci began to percolate. It was during a later trip to Europe with his future wife, Liana Davis, that Michael got a gentle nudge.

He explained: "We were in Vienna eating gelato one night. [Many Italian *gelatai* have shops in Austria.] And I said, 'Have I ever told you that I had the idea of opening a gelato shop in Mill Valley?'

"She said, 'No, you never mentioned that.'

"'Well, I've had the idea for a few years, just sitting in the back of my head.'

"She said, 'Why haven't you done anything about it?'

"'I don't know.'

"So we went back to the States and she kind of pushed me. 'Why don't you explore your idea a little bit? What do we have to do? What's the next step?'

"I definitely needed a partner to help me—it's too much to carry on one person's shoulders. And I already knew there were manufacturers of gelato equipment with schools in the States. So I figured that would be a really good jumping off point, to find out if this was something feasible for Liana and me," continued Michael.

He enrolled in an intensive course put on by Carpigiani (an Italian manufacturer of ice cream and gelato equipment) in North Carolina. It covered everything from creating a business plan to running a shop and making gelato, and ran five days from 9 AM to 6 PM.

"Afterward, we had dinner with the people teaching the course and our classmates, about a dozen of us talking gelato the whole time. So really, the school went until 10 or 11 at night. I met a lot of people who became key to our opening, such as the ex-president of Carpigiani USA and some people who design and build cafés," said Michael.

And so, Michael dived head first into gelato. The school finished in November, and by January, he and Liana headed to Rimini for a big gelato trade show, where they rubbed

elbows with the Italian world of gelato. He came away with a realization that things were drifting in the wrong direction. Even in Italy, where there are superb *gelatai* who make everything from scratch, with only seasonal fruit, there are also many who cut corners using powder to make the base and fruit syrup for flavoring, and pedal it, shamelessly, to tourists as *gelato artigianale*. (The vendors of mixes and syrup claim that fresh fruit doesn't have enough flavor.) Luckily, most Italians still appreciate the real thing.

"We decided to make gelato from scratch because there is no shortcut for the quality we wanted," said Michael. Ironically, it was a sales rep for a company selling gelato flavoring and mixes that became a great resource. "He lives outside Venice. His family includes three generations of gelato makers, and he helped us in developing recipes. We were able to use his knowledge for making our own base." This speaks well of Michael, because in Italy, the old-time gelato recipes are often top secret. A *gelataio* would go to his grave before revealing one.

And so, in June 2007, Michael and Liana opened Noci (no-chee) in Mill Valley, where his paternal grandmother Cecilia or Cici settled in the late 1940s. Initially, she migrated to the United States from Le Marche (on the central Italian coast south of Venice), landing in Michigan in the 1920s and marrying Michael's Italian-born grandfather, who worked as a miner.

A Dublin-born Irishman named John Reed was the first Anglo-Saxon settler in the Mill Valley region. He went to sea at a young age, and after sailing to Acapulco, where he lived for six years and learned fluent Spanish, he made his way to Los Angeles and then Yerba Buena (early San Francisco). He became friends with the commandant of the Yerba Buena presidio, Jose Antonio Sanchez, and eventually married his daughter Hilaria.

Reed became a Mexican citizen in 1834, which qualified him for land grant status; consequently, he received the first Mexican land grant north of San Francisco Bay, for an area that included Tiburon, Belvedere, and sections of Mill Valley and Corte Madera. After establishing a rancho, he built a lumber mill and exported lumber across the bay to help build the new presidio. It was Reed's mill that gave Mill Valley its name. (The mill site and replica is located in Old Mill Park near the town center.)

Things were going well for Reed—he and Hilaria had four children and the rancho and mill prospered. However, in the spring of 1843, he came down with a high fever. Bloodletting, still held in high esteem by the medical community, was the core of his treatment, and, as a result of a severed artery, he bled to death—at the young age of 38.

Mill Valley continued to be an agricultural and logging community until 1889, when the North Pacific Coast Railroad expansion into town and the ensuing land auction of 1890—by the Tamalpais Land & Water Company, an agency of the San Francisco Savings & Union Bank—brought families and businesses into the area. It became a summer vacation destination for affluent San Franciscans escaping the eternal summer fog. Many built summer homes in and around the town.

Also, the Mt. Tamalpais & Muir Woods Scenic Railway, billing itself as "The Crookedest Railroad in the World," opened in 1896, and carried many tourists to the top of nearby Mt. Tam, as the locals call it. The railroad ceased in 1930, wiped out by the 1929 fire and the Great Depression. Both this railroad and the passenger line to the San Francisco Ferry in Sausalito operated from Depot Plaza. Today, the plaza is a pleasant spot with a bookstore/café (the converted depot building) and outdoor tables.

By 1940, the recent opening of the Golden Gate Bridge (1937), along with the increasing popularity of the automobile, killed the passenger/commuter train service. And around 1960, the small, quiet bedroom community of Mill Valley started to grow and slowly morph into a very affluent upscale suburb. During the 1980s and 1990s, many mom and pop businesses disappeared, to be replaced with boutiques, art galleries, and upscale food stores.

Noci, however, remains very much a family affair, with Michael, the *gelataio*, in the kitchen and Liana running the front and acting as taster—"she has a really good palate"—and Michael's dad working as prep assistant in the kitchen. "He helps me every day," said Michael. "He'll be here later to cut strawberries and process blackberries. And he helps wash dishes and keep the kitchen clean."

Michael uses fresh, local, organic fruit in his gelato whenever possible. During the summer, he doesn't look further than Marin County and the Bay Area in general for strawberries, raspberries, peaches, nectarines, and juicy melon. The winter is a little different. Out of necessity, his citrus fruit comes from Southern California and Texas.

"We try to develop relationships with the local farmers, where we can call them and ask them questions. 'How is everything? What are the best tasting strawberries and raspberries?'" said Michael.

Noci's flavors are seasonal, so don't expect to find strawberry gelato in the winter. "This is hard for some of our customers to wrap their minds around, because here in America we're used to getting whatever we want, whenever we want—even if it has to be flown in from thousands of miles away," Michael explained.

His uncompromising artisan approach includes roasting California hazelnuts, almonds, and pistachios and grinding them to paste, as well as scraping his own vanilla beans for pure vanilla flavoring. In addition, he makes his own gelato base from milk, cream, eggs, and sugar—a time-consuming process.

A few Noci customers have helped Michael develop certain flavors—acting as tasters as they give him feedback and he makes changes, such as adding sugar, adding cream, or cooking the fruit. Sometimes cooking the fruit deepens the flavor (other times it becomes bland).

One customer in particular helped Michael with his coconut gelato. "It was too icy, too crumbly, had too many coconut chunks in it," he explained. "She would come often and taste my progress. Because she was Thai, she grew up with the flavor and knew it." He worked with her on a dozen batches of coconut over the course of two months, until he created a product that pleased them both.

As for sorbet (basically water, sugar, and fruit), Michael prefers plum, mango, and papaya because they're very fibrous, which helps maintain a creamy texture. Sorbet made from lemons and fruit with less fiber and more juice tend to become a huge icicle.

One difference between the gelato market here and in Italy is the flavors that customers prefer. Michael and Liana sell a lot of vanilla, strawberry, chocolate, and chocolate chip, while the Italians like *nocciola* (hazelnut), *bacio* (chocolate and hazelnut), *pistacchio*, and *riso* (rice).

The interior design of Gelateria Noci reflects Michael's hands-on approach with his gelato. He created all his own architectural drawings. "I knew what I wanted and the space I had, so we designed it to suit our needs," he said. He also made the granite counter, cabinets, and tabletops. The back counter, espresso machine, grinder, display case, chairs, and table legs all came from Italy. Noci feels cool, clean, and comfortable—you'll be inclined to choose your gelato, slurp, linger, and look at the art.

There's always a revolving art show on Noci's walls. The displays are varied—everything from kites, comic book art, and paintings on bamboo to a display of hand-painted bicycle frames, photos of a Cristo & Jean-Claude umbrella installation, and acrylics on canvas by Helen Steele. Both Liana (Masters in art history) and Michael (degree in graphic design) felt strongly from the beginning that a mini art gallery would be part of their gelateria.

Although relatively young, this cute couple goes way back. "I grew up two blocks down the street, and Liana grew up in Tam Valley," said Michael. "So we both went to Mill Valley Middle School. We met there, and were each other's first kiss [very sweet]. Then we went our separate ways. We got reacquainted again and started dating when she was getting her Masters at UC Davis, and I was just back in the area after a six-week cycling vacation in New Zealand."

Cycling was his passion before owning a gelato shop. Now, there isn't much time for pedaling—a definite sacrifice for a guy who says, "If it's got two wheels, I'll ride it." Not to worry, he's created his own Noci *bici* (bike)—a two-wheeled gelato cart that can handle two 50-pound coolers. He had the custom-designed bike made by SyCip, an artisan handbuilder of bicycles in Santa Rosa, and he wheels it around the neighborhood like the Mill Valley version of the Good Humor man.

Sometimes good humor visits Noci. In fact, there was a little girl (a regular) who came in with two friends. One of them had never been to Noci.

"I want *fior di latte*," said the first little girl.

And the new little girl asked, "What is that?"

"It's deliciousness."

Michael was so taken with this little vignette that his tagline on the ice cream board reads, "Less fat plus less air equals deliciousness."

Noci is still in its infancy, and every day the deliciousness of its gelato improves.

It was a women's shoe store; now it's a gelateria. The owners Michael and Liana are, more or less, self-taught and make damn good gelato—everything from scratch, with mostly organic ingredients. Here's a partial flavor lineup: stracciatella *(vanilla with chocolate shavings),* cookies n cream, cioccolato scuro *(dark chocolate),* caramello, marzipan, vaniglia bianca, noce di cocco *(coconut,) and* fior di latte *(cream). The couple is involved in the Slow Food Movement and was chosen as delegates to a recent Slow Food International gathering. (Slow Food describes itself as "a non-profit, eco-gastronomic member-supported organization that was founded in 1989 to counteract fast food and fast life.) Tourists, transplants, and locals patronize the place. Robin Williams comes in from time to time, as does Minnie Driver. So visit, grab a cone or cup, and walk around downtown Mill Valley.*

Emporio Rulli Larkspur

464 Magnolia Avenue
Larkspur
(415) 924-7478
7AM—5:30PM, Monday to Friday
7:30AM—5:30PM, Saturday & Sunday
Closed Thanksgiving and Christmas Day
www.rulli.com

For more Emporio Rulli, see pages 14–18.

*I*t's hard to imagine that Gary Rulli started his career deep frying doughnuts in a mini-market. But that part-time job during high school helped him pay for his very cool Super Sport Camaro—and discover his passion.

"I actually enjoyed doing it," said Gary. As a result, his Italian-born maternal grandfather, Nicola, asked old friend Gianni DiStefano, co-owner of Victoria Pastry Co., one of North Beach's Italian bakeries, to give his grandson a job. Gianni (and partners Romano Buoncristiani and Lorenzo Lavezza) said yes, but only after the kid had a little more experience.

Gary was always proud of his grandparents, both immigrants from Abruzzo, who arrived in California at the turn of the 19th century and eventually settled in Calistoga where they ran an inn. A man of many talents, Nicola earned a degree in architecture, became mayor of Calistoga, and sang with the chorus of the San Francisco Opera.

When Gary graduated from Marin Catholic, he applied for the apprenticeship program at Lafayette Pastry in San Francisco, and studied under Swedish pastry chef Bo Brink. Also, former owner Henry Arrigotti (from Torino) showed Gary the ins and outs of panettone and Italian biscotti. "The more I did it, the more I liked it. Eventually, I knew enough to start

working at Victoria Pastry a couple days a week," said Gary. "I had to prove myself because that's how they teach you in Italy. They want to see heart, not just talent."

The next big turning point came during a trip to Italy with his grandparents. "It was an eye-opening experience. Besides meeting the relatives, I went to Torino. I went to Milan. I went to Florence. I saw all these cafes and pastry shops. I thought, oh my god! This could be an incredible career," he said. In Italy, good pastry chefs are considered artists.

When Gary returned from Italy, his mission in life became very clear: he would learn how to make those marvelous Italian pastries. There were, however, some problems to overcome. He didn't speak Italian. And he had no contacts in the world of Italian pastry, outside of an introduction to Pietro Ferrua, owner of the famous Galup panettone factory. In the meantime, Gary worked at Victoria Pastry for a year and a half, until finally, he said, "I just decided to go."

The 21-year-old arrived in May 1982, staying with an old-fashioned aunt (his curfew was 8PM), and working a little at Galup in Pinerolo, outside of Torino. By the end of the summer, Gary still had not found a pastry school, plus he discovered that as a *straniero* (foreigner) he could only reside in Italy for three months without a *permesso di soggiorno* (a permit to stay and work for up to two years).

During a trip to Milan, he came across a beautiful and modern pastry shop called Pasticceria Piave. Owner Silvano Lulini, a talented pastry chef and cake decorator, agreed to bring Gary on as an apprentice. At the same time, Gary enrolled in a specialized pastry course for experienced people at CAPAC, a top polytechnic school in Milan, attending class three nights a week. He planned to return home at Christmas for his *permesso*. (In Italy, things often work backwards. A foreigner starts a job or school and then goes home to get a work permit from the Italian Embassy.)

"So I moved from Torino to Milan, and lived more or less in the warehouse. I slept in this little room with no running water. It was definitely a European apprenticeship. Every night I had dinner with his family. I'd work from 7AM until 11 at night. Silvano also did these huge catering events for Armani and Valentino. It was a great opportunity, because there were so many things that he didn't have time to do. Eventually, I'm making all the cakes for the window," explained Gary.

He went home at Christmas, got the *permesso*, and was set—except for one thing. "A month or two before I left [in May], I met Jeannie, my wife, while dancing at the Embarcadero, and we started writing letters, and even before I went to Italy we were pretty much in love."

After a year and a half, Gary returned to the Bay Area (and Jeannie) and decided to go into business for himself instead of returning to Victoria Pastry. "I wanted to put what I'd learned into production," explained Gary. "I wanted to use what I knew, because if a few years go by, I'm going to start forgetting things."

He had his heart set on opening an Italian café in San Francisco, but no one would give him a lease because it was the early 1980s and the economy was booming. In the meantime, he rented space in a pie company and sold wholesale pastries to restaurants including Modesto Lanzone, Fior d'Italia, and Fabrizio.

While delivering pastry to Fabrizio, in Larkspur, in Marin County, Gary noticed a storefront for lease and talked to the landlord. Originally, a restaurant called 464 Magnolia occupied the space; the chef was Michael Goldstein. It had been at the forefront of the California cuisine movement, until it was sold and eventually closed. The kitchen infrastructure was there, so Gary and Jeannie went for it. They cobbled together $150,000 from their savings and a loan on his parent's home, and completely remodeled the interior. Pasticceria Rulli opened for business on Thanksgiving Day, 1988.

Gary said, "I'd never done a business and neither had my parents. I didn't really have a mentor. No one to tell me even how to set up the books. We just kind of winged it."

The first three or four years in Larkspur proved rough going. Downtown was very quiet—almost like a ghost town. All the action took place at the doughnut shop across the street. In fact, some of its patrons were saying, "We give him 12 months and he's going to close." Years later, the people in the insurance agency next door to the doughnut shop told Gary, "We were taking bets in the office on how long you were going to last."

Even one of Gary's pastry chefs had his doubts. "This Frenchman was working for me. Jean Luc—I'll always remember—very, very French. After being open one year, he was telling me in a thick French accent, 'You know, Ga-ry, sometime you have to admit when you make the mistake. You know, some time it just do not work out.' He used to wear glasses and they would be full of flour so he couldn't see. He was like a caricature of a French pastry chef," said Gary.

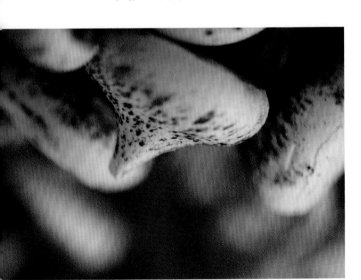

Eventually it *did* begin to work out. Larkcreek Inn changed hands and nationally renowned chef Bradley Ogden came in to run the kitchen. That put Larkspur on the map. From there, Gary's dream began to take off—and Jeannie's dream also, because, as they say in the pastry kitchens of Italy, "*L'altra metà della pasticceria e' la moglie* (the other half of the pastry shop is the wife)." With a background in graphic design, Jeannie's vision is reflected in the look of things—such as product packaging, chocolate boxes, display cases, and the Rulli catalogue.

The next big move came when Gary bought the brick building that included his shop and a bookstore. One thing he learned in Italy (and also in North Beach) was the concept of *comperar le mura*, which translates to "to buy the walls." The Italians have a long-term mentality that says: If I'm going to spend a million dollars to make a shop beautiful, I want to own the place and not get squeezed out eventually by high rents. Anything less is a handicap.

"Here, the attitude is do it as cheap as you can and make your money—because if they kick you out with a rent increase, you're not leaving anything in the building. I figured I was going to be a pastry chef for 40 or 50 years, and I wanted to own the building," said Gary.

By 1993, Gary had expanded from one storefront to three and started roasting his own coffee.

"I thought it would be really cool to have our own espresso blend," he explained. "Somebody I knew said if you want to learn how to coffee roast, you should talk to Alfred Peet, the guru of coffee. He's retired and doing some consulting.

"I met him and we hit it off. He reminded me of the pastry chefs I apprenticed with—in their late 60s or 70s—very European, very old school. Their approach was… this is how it is, and that's it. But I like that. He really took me under his wing. He was very impressed with the attention to detail and the quality of our pastry."

Alfred Peet was a pioneer in specialty coffee roasting who got people to think past percolated and stewed office coffee, which he considered swill. The son of a Dutch coffee roaster, he immigrated to San Francisco in 1955 at the age of 35. Eleven years later, he opened the first Peet's Coffee & Tea in Berkeley, California, at the corner of Walnut and

Vine, peddling dark roasted high-quality coffee to the public. Peet's garnered a following, and Alfred eventually sold his business (comprising three stores) in 1979. Along the way, he taught the original owners of Starbucks how to roast coffee. Peet's now has about 150 shops, mostly located in California. Alfred Peet passed away in 2007.

Gary put a coffee roaster in the kitchen and stacked sacks of green coffee beans in the corner of the café. As the espresso roasted, its seductive smell drifted into the street—similar to what happened in Rome 50 years ago, when many small cafés roasted their own coffee. They often piped the seductive aroma under doors or windows onto the sidewalk to draw people inside.

From Alfred Peet, Gary learned how to select the best coffees and roast them properly. Peet's is a very dark roast blend using more acidic, higher-altitude coffees from Costa Rica, Guatemala, Papua New Guinea, and Kenya. This blend works fine in drip coffee; however, an espresso machine accentuates the acidity.

Because of this, and the fact that he favors the Italian-style, medium roast blends, Gary toned down Alfred Peet's roasting style. He

uses the sweeter low-altitude Brazilian, Colombian, or Mexican coffee as a base, adding a touch of the more acidic beans for flavor. The result is, he says, "a beautiful smooth espresso."

"I'd go back to Italy every year and taste espresso there," explained Gary. "I'd put Brazil in the blend and Alfred would say, 'Not Brazil, the coffee's not good. It's not a great coffee.' Of course, I don't want to tell him what to do. But I had read Dr. Illy's book and done a lot of research and talked to coffee roasters in Italy. It's funny, because in the end Alfred loved our espresso blend."

The Dr. Illy that Gary refers to is the late Dr. Ernesto Illy of illycaffè S.p.A., the high-end Italian coffee brand. His father, Francesco Illy (a Hungarian serviceman who settled in

Trieste after World War I) started a coffee production and sales company in 1933. Dr. Illy, a trained biochemist, stepped in to run the company in 1963 and remained at the helm until 2004, when his son Andrea took over. Over the years, Dr. Illy gained the reputation as a scientific perfectionist and evangelist of espresso (also called Espresso Doctor and Papa Bean). Both Dr. Illy and Andrea produced books on espresso production, and collaborated on *Espresso: The Chemistry of Quality*.

"I picked it up very fast because pastry and coffee roasting are very close. It's all about feel. If you put puff pastry in a too hot oven, it explodes, and the inside is raw. And if it is not hot enough, the puff pastry doesn't develop. At the right temperature, it comes up, bakes all the way through, and is beautiful to eat. The same with coffee, you don't want to scorch the coffee, then it's raw inside and you taste all the weird flavors. If you under roast it, it has a sour taste. When it's done just right, you caramelize it and develop all the sugars, and you get a sweet espresso," said Gary, who did the roasting for ten years in the Larkspur kitchen. He now rents a warehouse in Greenbrae and uses a big new roaster to keep up with demand.

Gary is always in the kitchen, with his staff of ten. He said, "I'll do wedding cakes—here and there a special cake—but now, more than anything else, I do the panettone, mix the cookie and the croissant dough, and oversee the production." The pastries that his kitchen produces are superb—not too sweet, not too heavy—very simple and always fresh, just like you find in Italy. Begin eating your way through them with the following: *budino di ricotta* (little boat-shaped, ricotta-filled pie), *pan dolce di colomba*, *bomboloni* (a lightly fried dough delight), *focaccia dolce mandorlata* or *focaccia dolce con frutti di bosco* (a tasty flat pastry with either almond paste or berries), and *focaccia dolce di Antonello* (fine Valrhona chocolate, walnuts, and pistachios). The latter is named after Antonello Angeleri, a warm, funny, rubbery-faced man, who roasted coffee for Gary and also worked as a barista in Larkspur. Unfortunately for all, Antonello had a stroke and a heart attack, passing away in May 2009.

You must also try the brioche—so authentic, if you close your eyes you'll think you're in Milano. Pair it with a Rulli espresso or cappuccino, and you'll swear you're in Milano.

What is Gary Rulli's specialty, you ask? The panettone—both his specialty and his *capolavoro* (masterpiece). This is the time-honored artisan version, as opposed to the common mass-produced panettone. You begin with a pinch of natural yeast starter from the *lievito madre* (mother yeast). Gary got his original batch of starter from master pastry chef Silvano Lulini of Pasticceria Piave (where Gary apprenticed), and smuggled it home on the plane.

Initially, Lulini told Gary, "You don't really want to learn this."

Gary replied, "Yeah, I do."

"No, you don't. You have to take care of this dough. It's like being married. It's like your wife."

He wasn't kidding. When making his panettone, Gary refreshes the starter with flour and water three times every four hours—that's 12 hours. Then, he mixes the first dough (flour, sugar, butter, and yeast) in the 16th hour. That proofs overnight. In the morning, he adds more sugar, flour, egg yolks, and creamery butter—along with best Italian candied orange peels and golden raisins. From there, it takes another 6 hours before it goes into the oven. This is a more than 30-hour process.

For the last 20 years, Gary was lucky enough to be mentored by maestro pasticciere Achille Brena from Ponte San Pietro in the province of Bergamo. Brena is considered one of Italy's panettone masters.

"It's the most difficult thing in pastry. You go by the recipe, and trial and error, and understanding the mother dough. During panettone production, the mother dough is the dominant factor. You have to work your life around her. It took me years to get it right," said Gary. And he did get it very right, because he is a perfectionist. His panettone is excellent—he makes it all year round, but the biggest periods are Easter or Christmas. Buy one of Gary's panettones, take it home, and eat it fresh with mascarpone cheese or toasted with a little butter.

Like many things in Italy, the origins of panettone, the Milanese Christmas bread, are a little vague (it appeared sometime in the 1500s). Following are three panettone legends—choose the one you like best.

The love story version involves Ugo, a handsome young hawk breeder in the Milanese court of Duke Ludovico Sforza. He loved the beautiful Adalgisa, daughter of local baker Toni; however, Toni's family did not approve. A hawk breeder in the ducal court was way higher in the social pecking order than a poor baker's daughter. This did not thwart Ugo—he snuck into the bakery at night to meet his love, where she helped her father. Unfortunately, the bakery had some problems—the apprentice baker got sick, another bakery opened nearby, and business went south. Ugo posed as an apprentice to help out, and into the bargain, decided to improve the dough for the *pane* (bread) by adding butter, candied citron, eggs, and raisins. Customers went crazy; this new bread was a monster hit. The bakery made lots of money, and Ugo could now justify his marriage to the daughter of Toni, the affluent baker. This *pane di Toni* (Toni's bread) saved the day.

A second tale focuses on a kitchen boy named Toni, serving in the court of Duke Ludovico Sforza. During a banquet, the cook burned the dessert and was terrified of the Duke's wrath. Toni approached and said that he had made a sweet loaf with leftover dough, butter, and candied fruit. He offered it to the desperate chef, who served the improvised sweet. A big hit! When the Duke asked what it was called, Toni replied that he hadn't thought of a name, yet. The Duke, summoning all his ducal power and cleverness, proclaimed that it would be called *pane di Toni*.

And finally, the nun's version tells of young Ughetta, who lived in a poor convent. She made a Christmas treat for her fellow nuns by adding sugar, butter, candied fruit, and raisins to the bread dough, and then carving a cross on the top as a blessing—thus creating the first panettone and adding a little pleasure to convent life.

Gary returns to Italy at least once a year to keep his game sharp. He attends pastry shows and continues to work with some of Italy's great pastry chefs. "They open up their kitchens and invite me to work with them for a couple weeks. I apprentice in different places, and that's how I build my repertoire," he explained. "I'm creating and passing on a tradition."

Gary Rulli is a class act, and so are his cafés and his Italian bar. If you're visiting Marin County, Emporio Rulli in Larkspur has got you covered. Downtown Larkspur is cute and simpatico—the café offers the real deal when it comes to Italian eats, from pastry to vino. The coffee is smooth, just like you get in Italy. Panini imbottiti (filled with salmon or fresh turkey) and pastry such as torta della nonna (a ricotta tart with orange peel) are great. And, your taste buds will rate the Rulli panettone "superb." By the way, Gary is the only American-born member of Italian descent of the Accademia Maestri Pasticceri Italiani, an elite Italian association of pastry chefs (the who's who, the crema of the crop). In the City, it's Rulli's Ristobar on Chestnut Street or the genuine Italian bar on Union Square. At San Francisco International Airport, you'll also find a Rulli outpost.

Mirella's Dolci

Civic Center Farmer's Market
San Rafael Civic Center
10 Avenue of the Flags
8AM–1PM, Sunday
8AM–1PM, Thursday (in good weather)

*Y*our landmark for locating Mirella's Dolci is the long, graceful Marin County Civic Center building. It was designed by architectural genius Frank Lloyd Wright, who said, "We know that the good building is not the one that hurts the landscape, but is one that makes the landscape more beautiful than it was before that building was built."

This is certainly the case here. The Civic Center fits in seamlessly with its surroundings, linking the soft crowns of three surrounding hills. It has a futuristic 1940s look, as though aliens (with a fabulous design sense) dropped it into place—although the administrative wing was completed in 1962, and the Hall of Justice with courtrooms in 1969. Unfortunately, Mr. Wright never saw them; he passed away at age 92 on April 9, 1959, at Taliesin West in Phoenix.

The Sunday farmer's market spreads out over the parking lot behind Wright's building. Mirella Bonissoni is just inside the main entrance, on the right. Look for the booth with "Mirella" written on the awning. If you get bit lost, not to worry. You'll wander among rows of organic produce, fresh baked goods, gourmet foods, art work, and artisan clothing—about 200 booths in all. (Civic Center is one of roughly 4,300 farmer's markets around the country.)

What will you discover at Mirella's booth? First of all, there's Mirella—an attractive, animated Italian lady who must be older than she looks because she has two sons: Lucca, 21, and Julian, 15. She comes from Bologna—*"Una citta culinaria di eccellenza* [city of culinary excellence]. Bologna has the best food in Italy," explained Mirella. (She's a little biased, as a Bolognese would be.)

Bologna's specialties include *tortellini in brodo* and *ragu alla Bolognese*, along with *le piedine*, an Italian flatbread made on a *piastra* (Italian hot plate), and *le raviole di San Giuseppe*. Every Italian city has a sweet dedicated to San Giuseppe, the patron saint of carpenters, whose feast day is March 19. According to Mirella, in Bologna that sweet is *le raviole* (not to be confused with *i ravioli*, the square-shaped, ricotta-filled pasta).

Mirella makes her own very yummy version of these half-moon crumbly cookies, filled with homemade peach, apricot, or raspberry jam. Her *raviole* are a *capolavoro* (masterpiece): rustic, simple, and not overly sweet. They go well with a cup of tea or coffee, as do many of the things she creates: *chichini* (little tea cakes with colored sugar bits), *amaretti*, and *crostantina*—a blackberry- or apricot-jam mini-tart. The buttery dough is a combination shortbread and piecrust. Her regular *ravioli* are also a *caplavoro*, especially the *spinaci e ricotta*, ricotta cheese and fresh cooked spinach in a delicate pastry shell—so good you can eat them without sauce.

"I go a lot by the seasons. I tend to make a lot of *le raviole* in the summer because there is fresh fruit for the *marmalata*," said Mirella. "I also invented these little flat biscotti called *tondini*, in a packet of five. *Tondino* means a round shape (like a coaster for a glass). They're good with gelato or strawberries."

You can also try her breakfast panino (eggs, prosciutto, and mozzarella)—or a selection from the rest of Mirella's panini lineup: prosciutto and mozzarella; tomato with mozzarella and pesto; grilled chicken with herbs, sweet red pepper; and mozzarella and eggplant.

Mirella's dolci are made from her own recipes—many of which she developed during her teen years. "I always liked to cook, especially sweets. On Sundays, from the time I was 12, I would always bake. Being Catholic, my parents were so strict. I couldn't go out,

so I had to do something. It became my hobby," she said. "I liked to cook. I was always helping in the kitchen and interested in cooking."

Mirella came to the Bay Area in 1982. "At that time, there was no work in Italy, no opportunity. It has changed now, but in those days, it was different," she explained. When Mirella first arrived, she lived in North Beach, and then moved to Marin County. Eventually, she worked as a private chef for a family. "For a long time, I cooked once a week for an entire day, and then put the portions in a container in the freezer, all kinds of Italian dishes. I created the menu," said Mirella.

She also began peddling Mirella's Biscotti (or *mandorlati*). These are not the twice-baked, hard-as-a-rock biscotti that you know, but instead the chewy kind found in Italy, made from eggs, flour, sugar, baking powder, and whole nuts (almonds, hazelnuts, pecans), and baked just once. Each region has its own special name for this sweet. It's *mandorlati* in Bologna and *cantucci* in Florence.

(You should know that in Italy, all cookies come under the *biscotti* umbrella. American bakers, however, have adopted the word *biscotti* [biscuits or cookies] and applied it only to their version of the familiar, elongated Italian sweet.)

After a while, Mirella said, "I needed to give all my time to the biscotti." She quit working as a family chef, and focused on marketing to the stores, as well as running her booth at the Civic Center Farmer's Market. Finally, after a discouraging and time-consuming retail effort, she concentrated solely on the farmer's market.

Mirella refers to herself as a *fornaio* (baker) rather than a *pasticciere* (pastry maker). The difference, according to her, is that the *pasticciere* makes soft, moist pastries and cakes with *crema* (custard) and *panna* (whipped cream), while the *fornaio* tends to create things that are dryer in texture, such as her *raviole*, *crostate*, and *tondini*. "The things that I make, you find in the *forno* (bakery) in Italy, not in a *pasticceria* (pastry shop)," she explains.

She now thinks of both Italy and the United States as home: "When I'm here I miss there, and when I'm there I miss here. An immigrant doesn't have a country. *Siamo metà* [We're divided]."

One of the things she likes about the old country is that Italians are still reluctant to cut corners with food. They recognize and appreciate natural products. "In Bologna, we make tortellini by hand, one at a time. I make all my *dolci* from zero, no premix. There is a lot of that around—just adding eggs and milk to a package. In Italy, when you try to sell premix products, it doesn't work. Here, a lot of people can't tell *fatto a mano* [hand made] from premix. Everyone looks for a shortcut so they can make more money. It's still not so much that way in Italy." You hear this again and again from Italians, and others struggling to produce quality products. Many Americans (not you, of course) seem to be more interested in quantity than quality. If it's cheap and you get lots of it, then it's good.

When you ask Mirella what she does after work, the answer is—there's no "after work," no down time. She's always in the kitchen making her goodies. It was different when she worked as a family chef. There was time to take classes in painting and sketching at the San Francisco Art Institute.

She followed up her art school studies with classes at the California School of Professional Fabric Design in Berkeley, founded by Zeida Rothman. (Rothman has some great textile design credits: Wamsutta Sheets, Fieldcrest Cannon, Burlington Industries, and Schumacher Fabrics and Rugs, along with a wide variety of men's, women's, and children's apparel. Rock star Elton John also called on her to design an original collection of fabrics for him.)

Stop at the Sunday Civic Center Farmer's Market in San Rafael (on your way north to the Wine Country), and look for Mirella's booth. You must try her moon-shaped, homemade jam-filled raviole, *her delicate* ravioli, *or her thin delicate* tondini. *Of course, you won't want to pass up her fresh lemonade—organic lemons, sugar, and water. It took Mirella a long time to perfect this drink, and if she's happy with it, it must be good. She's very fussy about all her products, from panini to dolci. How's your Italian? Go ahead and practice on Mirella. In the meantime, here are a few Italian proverbs from her website:* Non e' bello cio' che e' bello, ma e' bello cio' che piace *(Beauty is not what is beautiful, but beauty is what you like).* Chi canta a tavola e mangia a letto, e' un matto perfetto *(Who sings at the table and eats in bed, is a perfect crazy person).* Quello che non strozza, ingrassa *(That which does not choke you, makes you fat).*

CAFÉ LISTINGS

Arizmendi Bakery   (pp. 106–115)
1331 9th Avenue
(415) 566-3117
7AM–7PM, Tuesday to Friday
7:30AM–6PM, Saturday
7:30AM–5PM, Sunday
Closed Monday
www.arizmendibakery.org

Axis Café   (pp. 170–179)
1201 8th Street
(415) 437-2947
8AM–9PM, Monday to Friday
10AM–3PM, Saturday to Sunday
www.axis-cafe.com

Bi-Rite Creamery & Bakeshop
    (pp. 26–33)
3692 18th Street (at Dolores)
(415) 626-5600
11AM–10PM, Sunday to Thursday
11AM–11PM, Friday & Saturday
www.biritecreamery.com

Blue Bottle
Kiosk   (pp. 38–49)
315 Linden Street (in Hayes Valley)
(415) 252-7535
7AM–5 or 6PM, Monday to Friday
8AM–5 or 6PM, Saturday & Sunday
www.bluebottlecoffee.net
Mint Plaza
66 Mint Street (corner of Jessie Street)
(415) 495-3394
7AM–7PM, Monday to Friday
8AM–6PM, Saturday
8AM–4PM, Sunday
www.bluebottlecoffee.net

Café Metropol   (pp. 18–27)
168 Sutter Street
(between Kearny Street and Lick Place)
(415) 732-7777
11AM–9PM, Monday to Friday
7AM–2PM, Saturday
Closed Sunday
www.cafe-metropol.com

Caffè Baonecci   (pp. 76–83)
516 Green Street
(415) 989-1806
10:30AM–9:30PM, Tuesday to Saturday
12PM–4:30PM Sunday lunch only
Closed Monday
www.caffebaonecci.com

Caffè Greco   (pp. 52–61)
423 Columbus Avenue
(415) 397-6261
7AM–11PM, Monday to Friday
7AM– midnight, Saturday & Sunday
www.caffegreco.com

Cavalli Café   (pp. 62–75)
1441 Stockton Street (at Columbus Avenue)
(415) 421-4219
11AM–11PM, Monday to Saturday
11AM–6:30PM, Sunday
www.cavallicafe.com

La Copa Loca   (pp. 153–159)
3150 22nd Street (at Capp Street)
(415) 401-7424
1PM–9PM, Monday
9AM–10PM, Tuesday to Saturday
10AM–9PM, Sunday
www.lacopalocagelato.com

Emporio Rulli Il Caffè   (pp.14–18)
On Union Square at Stockton and Post streets
7:30AM–7PM, daily
Closed Thanksgiving and Christmas Day
www.rulli.com

Emporio Rulli Larkspur   (pp. 201–212)
464 Magnolia Avenue
Larkspur
(415) 924-7478
7:00AM——5:30PM, Monday to Friday
7:30AM——5:30PM, Saturday & Sunday
Closed Thanksgiving and Christmas Day
www.rulli.com

Java Beach Café   (pp. 94–105)
Near Golden Gate Park
1396 La Playa Street (at Great Highway)
(415) 665-5282
5:30AM–11PM, Monday to Friday
6AM–11PM, Saturday & Sunday
www.javabeachcafe.com

Java Beach Café   (pp. 94–105)
At the San Francisco Zoo
2650 Sloat Boulevard (at 45th Avenue)
(415) 731-2965
5:30AM–11PM, Monday to Friday
6AM–11PM, Saturday & Sunday
www.javabeachcafe.com

Liguria Bakery   (pp. 84–91)
1700 Stockton Street (at Filbert)
(415) 421-3786
8AM–2PM, Monday to Friday
7AM–2PM, Saturday
7AM–noon, Sunday

Mirella's Dolci   (pp. 213–219)
Civic Center Farmer's Market
San Rafael Civic Center
10 Avenue of the Flags
8AM–1PM, Sunday
8AM–1PM, Thursday (in good weather)

Mission Beach Café   (pp. 134–143)
198 Guerrero Street (at 14th Street)
(415) 861-0198
7AM–10PM, Monday to Thursday
7AM–11PM, Friday
9AM–11PM, Saturday
9AM–6PM, Sunday
www.missionbeachcafesf.com

Mojo Bicycle Café   (pp. 116–123)
639-A Divisadero Street
(415) 440-2370
7AM–10PM, Monday to Wednesday
7AM–midnight, Thursday & Friday
8AM–midnight, Saturday
8AM–5PM, Sunday
www.mojobicyclecafe.com

Noci   (pp. 192–200)
17 East Blithedale Avenue
Mill Valley
(415) 388-2423
11:30AM–9PM, Sunday to Thursday
11:30AM–10PM, Friday & Saturday
www.nocigelato.com

Philz Coffee   (pp. 160–167)
3101 24th Street (at Folsom Street)
(415) 875-9370
6AM–8:30PM, Monday to Friday
7AM–8:30PM, Saturday & Sunday
www.philzcoffee.com

Piccino Café & Coffee Bar   (pp. 180–189)
Corner of 22nd Street and Minnesota Street
(415) 824-4224
Café
11AM–9:30PM, Tuesday to Friday
10AM–9:30PM, Saturday & Sunday
Closed Monday
Coffee Bar
7AM–5PM, Monday to Friday
8AM–5PM, Saturday & Sunday
www.piccinocafe.com

Ristobar   (pp. 14–18)
2300 Chestnut Street (at Scott Street)
(415) 923-6464
5PM–10PM, Monday to Thursday
5PM–11PM, Friday & Saturday
5PM–10PM, Sunday
www.ristobarsf.com

Ritual Coffee Roasters   (pp. 144–152)
1026 Valencia Street
(415) 641-1011
6AM–10PM, Monday to Friday
7AM–10PM, Saturday
7AM–9PM, Sunday
www.ritualroasters.com

Samovar Tea Lounge   (pp. 28–37)
Yerba Buena Gardens, Upper Terrace
730 Howard Street
(415) 227-9400
10AM–8PM, Sunday to Wednesday
10AM–9PM, Thursday to Saturday
www.samovarlife.com